ON THE OTHER SIDE

The powerful story of one woman's struggle through guilt, shame, and remorse after having two abortions, and how she found forgiveness, healing, and real love—the love of Jesus.

CHRISTY TAYMAN

ISBN 979-8-89345-240-2 (paperback)
ISBN 979-8-89345-241-9 (digital)

Christian Faith Publishing
832 Park Avenue
Meadville, PA 16335
www.christianfaithpublishing.com

Printed in the United States of America

DEDICATION PAGE

I dedicate this book to Jesus, my Lord and Savior, who asked me to write this book and who gave me the words. For His glory, I know that anyone who seeks Him will find forgiveness and salvation, healing and blessings - in His name.

CHAPTER 1

It was a frigid, cold February day in Montana. The streets were snow covered and slick. My mother almost canceled her doctor's appointment that day. She was scheduled for a regular monthly pregnancy checkup, but the weather could get even worse over the next few days, so she headed to the doctor's office.

The doctor said I was dead. He could not hear a heartbeat. When my mother told him that she had not felt the baby move in the last couple of days, the doctor became extremely concerned and sent her to the hospital, where they immediately induced labor. I was born that evening—three months early. This was in 1954, when premature babies born three months early rarely survived. They did not have neonatal nurseries or specialized equipment to assist premature babies to breathe or finish developing. The doctor discovered a long piece of the umbilical cord had almost rotted through. I was not getting the nourishment and oxygen to sustain my life. My parents were told that I would not have lived through the night if they had not induced labor when they did. The doctors and nurses were doing everything possible for their tiny new baby girl.

There was a registered nurse in the newborn nursery, at the hospital where I was born, who was well-known around the state for her incredible skills in saving premature babies. She had been featured in several newspaper articles with pictures of the tiny newborn babies when she had helped to save their lives. I have always thought of her as God's secret weapon. When the doctor pulled me into this world three months before I was supposed to be born, he handed me to that remarkable woman; she was my grandmother.

I was kept in the nursery for quite a while, under my grandmother's care, before my parents were allowed to finally bring me home. That is when I met my big brother for the first time. He was two and a half years old and was destined to become my hero.

My parents were married after my mother had dropped out of high school when she was just sixteen years old. My grandmother told me they agreed to allow her to get married that young because they were certain she was going to end up pregnant if they did not. She was a sophomore when she dropped out and married my father; he had already graduated and was several years older than my mother. They moved into a small one-bedroom basement apartment, and a year later, she had my brother. When she got pregnant again, my father, his brother, and my grandfather, along with some other friends, built us a new house. To pay for it, my father worked two jobs so my mother could stay home and take care of the babies.

My father was a mechanic and ran a full-service station during the day. He would come home and eat dinner, take a shower, and go to his second job, where he was the manager of the Anaconda Company's employees' club. They had a golf course, bowling alley, café, gym for intramural basketball and dances, and a bar. As soon as the bar closed at 2:00 a.m., he would head home to bed.

Some of my earliest memories are with my father, working in our garage, with his buddies, on one of their hot rods or motorcycles. My father's brother was a city policeman and was a motorcycle officer during the summer months. Both my father and my uncle had motorcycles and rode with a group of friends. My uncle would let me ride in front of him on his personal motorcycle, and he would take me for rides up and down our street. I loved riding motorcycles and wasn't afraid of them.

The group would take off for a weekend together and camp in the mountains somewhere. I remember they all went to Glacier National Park one summer. My grandmother packed up her station wagon and took my brother and me along with all the food. We roasted hot dogs over a big campfire and then got the marshmallows out and made s'mores. My grandmother and brother and I slept in the back of the car that night. The next morning, we ate breakfast cereal right out of the little single-serving boxes you could open and pour milk in. I was four years old on that trip.

Before my mother got pregnant with my brother, she and my father joined the group and rode motorcycles a lot. After I was born, my father worked long hours and was away from home from early morning until late at night. My mother told me she felt like she missed all the fun she was supposed to have growing up as a teenager. She said she was lonely and tired of playing house, and she hated being stuck there taking care of two whiny little kids.

My mother was the most selfish, self-centered person I ever met. She was mean and had a temper and took her frustrations out on my brother and me. I learned very early to stay away from Mommy when she got mad because she would hit us if we were standing close to her. My brother told me she hit him so hard once that he smacked his head. He got sick and threw up, so she took him to the hospital. He had a concussion. I was still a baby, so I do not remember that time, but there was another time when we were ice-skating. She pushed him, trying to get him to skate out onto the ice. He fell hard and hit his head. He crawled into the back seat of the car and started throwing up. That was another concussion.

My brother and I both displayed behaviors from the environment of abuse, stress, and anxiety we lived in with our mother. My brother sleepwalked and had terrible nightmares. Our mother told us we could never leave our bedrooms after she put us to bed. If we had to go to the bathroom, we had to stand at our bedroom door and call her for permission. If we forgot and she caught us out of our rooms, we got spanked. We figured out that she used to leave us alone many nights; she got dressed up and went out with her girlfriends to the bars, drinking and dancing. She knew when our father would get home, and she would come running in and jump into bed before he arrived.

One night I had called and called, and she never came. I was sitting on the floor at my bedroom doorway, crying, when my big brother said, "She's not here. Go ahead and go to the bathroom. I will watch and let you know if she comes." I ran to the bathroom and back to my bed as fast as I could. She never came, so we figured she was gone again.

When my brother had a bad nightmare, he would scream until someone woke him up. I remember many nights hollering for my mother to come and help him, but she never came. I would sneak around the corner into my brother's room and wake him up. He would be terrified and crying and would ask me to check under the bed to make sure there was not a monster under there. I would pull the blankets up and show him that there was not anything under his bed, so he was safe. Sometimes he would ask me to check in the closet. I would go over and open the closet door and show him there were not any monsters in the closet. He would be terrified and did not want to be alone, so I'd crawl into bed with him, and we would fall asleep.

Many nights, my daddy would find me when he got home and take me back to my own room. I would tell him about the bad dreams and how Mommy never came to help when I called for her. He would tuck me back into my bed and kiss me good night, and he would call me kitten; he said when I was born, I was the same size as a kitten in his hands.

The day came when my big brother started school, and I had to stay home. I was devastated and missed him terribly. I asked over and over if I could go to school with him. It was very difficult for me to be alone. One day after he had gone to school, my mother got very sick. My father was at work, so I was at home alone with my mother. She started to lie down on her bed, but something was wrong. She fainted, and she had blood on her legs. I called her and shook her, but she did not move or say anything.

I knew my grandmother's phone number and called her. It was just lucky she wasn't working that day and was at home to take the call. I told her Mommy had blood on her legs and she would not wake up. My grandmother said to sit right there, that she was on her way. She said she was going to call the ambulance and, if they got there first, that I was to let them in and show them where my mother was.

When the ambulance got to our house, I opened the door and took them back to the bedroom where my mother was still unconscious. My grandmother arrived just as they were putting my mother into the ambulance. I found out years later that I saved my mother's life that day. She had an ectopic pregnancy and was hemorrhaging. If I had not reached my grandmother, my mother would have bled to death. They did not have 911 yet, and at four years old, the only phone number I knew was my grandmother's.

Eventually, I also went to school. I loved school. I loved playing with the other children; but mostly, I loved reading the books, the colors, the maps, and learning how to print the alphabet. I took to school like a duck to water. And I got to go to the very same school that my big brother was at. I would see him across the playground at recess. I knew he had friends who were older than me whom he wanted to be with. The rule on the playground was the younger kids were not to bother the older kids. It was enough to see him playing softball or kickball. I knew he was close.

He taught me how to play marbles so he could practice at home with me. Someone would draw a big circle in the dirt, and then two kids got down and shot at each other's marble. Whoever knocked the other marble out of the circle first won that marble.

One day, I was playing with an older boy. He was acting tough and like it was silly to play with a little girl, but he got down and challenged me. I was fairly good and won a couple of marbles. Then he got out his steelie, a solid silver marble that everyone tried to win. They were heavier and harder to knock out of the circle, and when you won one, you kept it. I tried my best, even got down in the dirt in my pretty little dress on my knees, and I finally knocked the steelie out of the circle. I won the steelie! But as quick as he could the kid grabbed up the steelie and several more of my marbles and ran off. The bell rang for the end of recess, and we all had to line up to go back into our classrooms.

I told my big brother what had happened when we got home that evening. He knew the boy and said he would get my marbles back for me. The next day, the boy brought me back my marbles and the steelie. He never bothered me again.

One day, after I had started first grade, our mother told us to pack our suitcases because we were going to stay with our grand-parents that weekend. We each had a small suitcase that we took to our grandparents when we got to spend the night. We knew something was wrong because our mother was mad and throwing things around. We were careful to be quiet and not ask any questions. It was just dusk when she pulled up in the alley behind our grandparents' house. She reached across the seat, opened the car door, and told us to get out and go into the house. While my brother opened the gate, I watched her drive away. I saw the red brake lights come on when she got to the street. She turned the corner and was gone. Our grandparents were eating dinner and did not know that we were coming. My mother disappeared for several months, and then she filed for divorce. My father was working both jobs and couldn't take care of two little kids, so we stayed with our grandparents.

My father had a tough time getting through the divorce. He and his whole family were Catholics, and at that time, the Catholic church did not accept divorce. My father's parents and their families let him know what a disgrace he was because no one had ever been divorced in their family before. At one point, my father attempted to take his own life.

Unable to handle things, he decided to move to another state. I was sitting in my first-grade classroom when I looked up, and there was my daddy at the door. Because we had been staying at our grandparents' home, we had not seen our father very much. He told the teacher, a Catholic nun, that he was moving out of state and did not know when he would be back. He asked if he could give me a hug before he left; the nun told him no and said that he had to leave because he was disturbing the class. I was standing by my desk, ready to run into his arms, but when she said no, I started to cry. I did not know where he was going, and I was scared because my teacher told him I could not go to him, that he was going to leave me there. I did not understand what was happening.

First, our mother left and did not want us, and now our father was leaving and obviously did not want us either because he was moving away but was not taking us with him. How does a six-year-old child handle that kind of rejection? I could not understand how our parents could just walk away from us like that. The more I worried about why they left, the more I became convinced that there must be something terribly wrong with me. My big brother was my hero, and I knew there was not anything wrong with him, so it had to be me. I was not sure what it was, but it had to be something terrible because neither my mommy nor my daddy wanted me.

I worried about this for my entire childhood. I was afraid my friends or my teachers could tell what it was, so I tried to get straight As in everything and never acted up in class. I did the best I could, knowing all along that there was something terribly wrong with me. When children tell themselves something like that over and over for years, it becomes very real to them.

After our parents left, we would visit our aunt and uncle, our mother's brother and his wife, at their ranch. Sometimes, my brother got to spend the weekend and would help our uncle with different chores. When I got a little older, I got to spend time there too. They had a girl who was six years younger than me, and she had a little brother two and a half years younger than her. Our little cousins were more like our little sister and brother because we were so close.

Our aunt and uncle were very kind to us and seemed more like a father and mother. My uncle took my brother fishing and hunting. My brother grew so close to our uncle as he got older and could do more things together. When I got older, I got to babysit my little cousins if my aunt had chores to do. I loved playing with them and reading books with them. We spent every birthday together with them and each of the holidays.

We did not hear from our parents very much. We never got any birthday gifts from them or even a card or a phone call. We never got Christmas gifts from them. Except for the tuition to attend the Catholic school those first few grades, they never sent any money to help buy us clothes or shoes or pay for doctors' bills or dentists' bills.

Some of the time, our mother lived in the same city, and we knew where she worked. One weekend, I got a wonderful surprise. She had seen how our grandmother fixed up a bedroom for my brother, with a bed and pine dresser that matched and a corner desk and chair. The whole room was decorated like it was a cabin in the mountains. They even put up a mural on the wall behind his bed that was a picture of the mountains with a creek flowing past. I thought it was really cool. Our mother had lived her whole life in the shadow of her brother, and it was no secret that our grandmother favored him over her. It was so obvious that my brother and I could even see how she treated him better than she did our mother. My bedroom had a small single bed with a little table and lamp and a small dresser. Nothing matched, but I did not think anything about it.

My mother looked at the obvious differences between our rooms, and she got mad. She went to a furniture store and picked out a beautiful white canopy bed that had pretty little pink roses painted across the headboard. There was a crisp white eyelet canopy that stretched over the top, and the bedspread was covered with pink roses. There was a beautiful white dresser that matched the bed and had the same pink roses painted down the front.

My grandparents did not know anything about this until the deliverymen arrived at the door. My grandmother was at work, so we were home with our grandfather. He took them upstairs and had to move the furniture that was in the room before they could set the bed up for us. I was so excited and felt just like a little princess. My grandmother told me years later when I was an adult that my mother had charged everything to my grandparents' account. They had to pay for the furniture, but my mother acted like she bought it for me. When my grandmother got home from work, I was sitting up on my pretty new bed. What could they do? They could not send it back after I had seen it, and it was in my room.

That was not the only time my mother did this. There was a neighborhood grocery store around the corner from our grandparent's house. They had an account there too. My grandmother would let my brother or me walk to the store if she needed a can of corn or some milk or something for fixing dinner. They knew us and would charge it on my grandparents' account. When my grandmother went to pay the account one time, she found it was over what it should have been. When they looked, there were several charges for steaks, roasts, pork chops, vegetables, and other groceries my grandmother had not bought. My mother was going in and charging for food for her and her husband. She never paid my grandmother back, but the couple who owned the grocery store agreed not to let her charge anything there again. My mother did the same thing at a small pharmacy that my grandmother had an account at and charged quite a bit before anyone caught it. It was these kinds of things that my mother did—and then she would lie about it—that continued to develop the hurt feelings between my grandparents and my mother.

My mother joined the Montana Cowgirls Association. She got my brother and me and took us out to a field on the edge of town. There was a beautiful horse that came up to us when we walked up to the gate. She told us she bought the horse, the saddle, saddle blanket, and the rest of the gear and that she was paying to rent the field and feed the horse. The Montana Cowgirls Association opened all the rodeos. They wore fancy fringed outfits and hats and carried the flags into the arena for the national anthem to be sung. Then they would do fancy riding and figure eights and put on a show to get the rodeo going. I remember my grandmother was angry at her for spending all that money but not offering to buy her own children clothes to wear.

One of the local Western-wear shops in town put on a fashion show of new Western clothes before the rodeo hit town. It was where my mother got her outfits for riding in the rodeos. I got asked to be a model in one of the shows when I was in the second grade. I got to keep the clothes that I wore for the show. I had a pair of jeans, a pretty flowered Western shirt with fringe and pearl snap buttons, a leather belt with a huge silver buckle, a straw hat with silver concho pieces around the brim, and brand-new cowgirl boots.

The show was held in one of the largest Western bars with a great big dance floor. For the fashion show, we had to walk around the circle of the dance floor. The new boots were slippery, and when I went to turn around in a circle, I flew around on the heel of my new boots. I stayed on my feet and kept walking, but there was a crowd of drunk cowboys at the table on the edge of the dance floor, and they whooped and hollered and clapped for me. The next time, I took the corner much slower and did not slip on the floor.

In 1962, the summer before I went into the fourth grade, my grandmother took us to the Seattle world's fair. We flew to Seattle; it was my first plane ride. It was a gray cloudy day when we took off, but when the plane got above the clouds, I was stunned. The brilliant sun was shining across these huge pillows of silvery clouds for as far as I could see. I thought we had popped into heaven, and I began to cry! The stewardess was so kind and brought my brother and me little pins of an airplane to wear. I could not stop staring out the window and loved it when the clouds parted, and I could watch the ground as we raced across the sky.

We landed in Spokane, Washington, and let some people get off the plane. My uncle was working at that airport and met the plane. He got to come on board for a few minutes to visit with us. It seemed like he was a particularly important person because the pilot spoke to him and then all the stewardesses, and they seemed proud that he was visiting their plane. He worked for the Federal Aviation Administration.

When we got to Seattle, we took a taxi from the airport to the hotel that was downtown. It took a long time to get there. Seattle was the biggest city that I had ever been to before. I was a little scared of the freeways because there were so many cars and trucks going so fast. I loved the tall buildings and have always been fascinated with them. I wondered what all the people in them were doing at that very moment. When we finally got to our hotel, we could see the Space Needle from the windows.

The next day, we rode on the monorail that had been built to get to the fairgrounds. These were simply wonderful things to see and enjoy. I remember all the colorful flags from all over the world, and there were so many places with incredible food, some from places I had never heard of.

My brother was most excited to get to see the display of $1,000,000. It was all one-dollar bills stacked up in a massive pile on a table. We could walk right up to it, but there were guards all around, and if you reached out to touch it, they let you know not to do that.

My favorite thing was getting to see the *Mona Lisa*, the actual original painting by Leonardo da Vinci. It was overwhelming to me to be standing in front of such a famous painting that had been created in the 1500s. I could have stood there all day just looking at it. There were guards posted on both sides of the painting, and they had a braided rope hung out across the front so you could not get too close to it. I will never forget it, and if I ever get the chance to travel to the Louvre in Paris, where it is kept now, I will visit her again.

Riding up into the Space Needle was fantastic. The elevators had a glass front so you could look out as you went up. I had never been in any building that tall before, and I loved it. Once we got to the top, my brother and I raced outside to look over the railing. We could see across the whole fairgrounds and watched the fountain squirt up from far below us. We were astonished that the café up there rotated around while we ate our lunch. We saw the docks and the ferry boats on Puget Sound, Lake Washington, and then all the fabulous skyscrapers again downtown. Going to the world's fair is something I have remembered my whole life with wonder and joy.

My mother married one of the cowboys she met, and for a while, they lived right there in the same city where we lived. He worked in construction, and she worked at different retail stores. He was an alcoholic, and when he drank, he became extremely violent. After one barroom brawl, he put several men in the hospital. Another time after he had been in a fight, he was sentenced to serve time in the state psychiatric hospital. My mother drove over every weekend to visit him. They got back together when he got out.

He would beat her when he got drunk. If her injuries were so bad that she had to go to the hospital, she would call my grand-mother and ask if she could come and stay there when she was released. Many times, I would get up and go downstairs to find her sleeping on the couch. Her face would be unrecognizable. It looked like raw, bloody hamburger. She would have teeth missing, her eyes were swollen closed, and her lips were split and swollen. She would have broken ribs, broken fingers, and bruises on her back and legs where he had kicked her. Sometimes she would have chunks of hair missing that he had pulled out by the handful. She would stay with us for a while, but she would always go back to him. I never under-stood that. I could not understand her choosing him and that life over her own children.

When they first got married, he asked if we wanted to come and live with them. Our grandmother knew about his drinking and fighting and refused to let that happen. My grandparents went to court and got my mother declared an unfit mother for abandoning us and offering no support for our care, and then they petitioned to adopt us so she could not take us. I remember the day they came home from court and showed us the paper that said we were now their children. They asked us if we wanted to take their last name or keep our own. We chose to keep our own.

He kept beating her, and she kept going back to him. They made the decision to move to Seattle, where his mother and sister and her family lived. Several years later, when we went back to Seattle for another vacation with our aunt and two cousins, they invited us to stay with them for a few nights. Shortly after we arrived, he began drinking. My grandmother and aunt got a taxi, and we quickly left. We stayed at a hotel, and my mother came to visit us the next day. We were going to the Seattle zoo, and I asked my mother if she would come with us. She said she could not do that and that she had to get back home. I asked her if she had come to have lunch with us. She said she could not and that she had to get right back home.

Again, I wondered why she chose him over seeing her own children and having an opportunity to be with them. And again, I was certain it was because there was something terribly wrong with me. That was the only thing that made sense to me.

When our parents left, my brother and I had been attending a Catholic school. My father had asked our grandparents to keep us in the Catholic school and to take us to Mass on Sundays because he wanted us to be raised Catholic. He had been sending them some money to pay for the tuition, but my father remarried and was having more children with his new wife. By the time I was in the fourth grade and my brother was in the sixth grade, our father had stopped sending any money to our grandparents. They were paying for our food, our clothes, and anytime we got sick and had to go to the doctor. Because they were not our parents, their insurance would not let them put us on their coverage, so things got tight. They decided to move us to public schools the following year.

At first, I was excited because the school was only a few blocks from our house, and I could easily walk back and forth to the fifth grade. But when school started that fall, I realized that I would not be going to the same school as my big brother, who would be attending seventh grade at the junior high school. He left for class earlier than I did, and I began to have serious problems.

I have never liked being left alone; my big brother was always there. We had been taking care of each other for as long as I could remember, and watching him walk out of the yard really upset me. My grandparents were at work and had hoped we were old enough to get ourselves up and out the door each morning. I had no problem getting ready. The problems started when I watched my brother disappear down the street, and I was left there alone. I cried and screamed and was terrified that I would never see him again. I only had forty-five minutes before I was to leave, but those forty-five minutes became a living hell for me every single day.

Our next-door neighbor lady heard me screaming one morning and came running over to find out what was wrong. I could not really tell her why I was so upset. I remember telling her over and over that my brother had just left for school, and I was all alone. I do not know if she ever understood, but she stayed with me until I calmed down and left for school.

She told my grandmother that evening when she got home from work. We talked about what a big girl I was now—in the fifth grade—and it was only forty-five minutes before I had to leave. She did not understand what the problem was. How does a ten-year-old child explain that she watched her mommy leave, then her daddy left, and she had always had her big brother at school, and now he was leaving too? How can a ten-year-old child tell someone that they were suffering the effects of being abandoned when she was six years old?

My grandmother arranged for me to leave when my brother left, and I walked half a block to a neighbor's house and waited there until I had to leave for school. They were a kind older couple whom I liked very much, so I was comfortable with them. I came to realize that my brother was going to be there when I got home from school and eventually no longer needed to spend the morning with the neighbors. I knew that whatever it was that was so wrong with me had caused me to be so scared when I was alone.

I enjoyed being in the fifth grade at the public school. The Catholic school had been a bit ahead in arithmetic, so I did well that year. I was always a good reader and enjoyed the program the public schools had for ordering books we could buy. My grandfather loved history and was always reading books about other times and places. He had taught us how important it was to try to understand how other people lived and what history taught us about them. He was a huge inspiration to my brother and me for reading all kinds of books.

When my grandmother was off during the week, I could walk home from school for lunch. On one warm autumn day, just a few weeks after I started the fifth grade, I was happily on my way home to have lunch with her. I noticed several boys were following me, but I thought they must be going home for lunch too. I was skipping along in my pretty little dress and white socks with lace and my brand-new shoes.

On the next block, the four boys had caught up with me and had begun to tease me, pulling the ribbons in my hair and flipping my skirt up so they could see my panties. I got mad and slapped one boy's hand away and told him to stop doing that. They were older than me, but my big brother always had friends around, so I really was not frightened yet.

One boy grabbed my arm and was holding on so tightly, I yelled at him. He did not let go. Another boy grabbed my other arm, and they made me fall to the ground. The third boy took a hold of one of my legs and was putting his hand under my skirt. I was crying and scared and did not understand what was happening. I was rolling from side to side and kicking with the leg nobody was holding. I kicked the fourth boy hard in the shins because he was just standing there, yelling at the other boys to hold me still. He got mad and tried to kick me back, but I had gotten one of my arms free and was swinging at the boy who had been holding it.

A neighbor lady came out of her house several doors down from where they had me on the sidewalk. She yelled, "What is going on?" She started across the street, and the four boys took off running. She helped me up and asked if I was all right. I said I was okay and that my house was just down the block.

I ran home to my grandmother. I was shaken and disheveled. My skirt was torn, and my new shoes were scraped up. My hair was a mess where they had pulled the ribbons out, and my elbow was bleeding. I started crying and tried to tell my grandmother what had happened. She kept asking me what the boys did to me. She pulled me up into her lap and rocked me like I was three years old again.

When I calmed down, we had lunch, and she said she would drive me back to school. I did not want to go back there. Nothing like that had ever happened to me at the Catholic school. I was certain that whatever it was that was wrong with me was why the boys had tried to hurt me. My grandmother was very stern about my returning to school; she walked me up to my classroom and promised that she would come and pick me up after school. Then she went down and had a talk with the principal. All four of the boys were called out of class. I did not know what was going on. All four of them were expelled.

Several days later, one of the other boys in my class came up to me at recess and made a comment about how I got them all expelled because they had tried to rape me. I did not know what rape was, so I just walked away. I had never heard that word before, and I needed to know what it meant. I asked one of the older girls from the sixth grade, and she explained it to me—that they were trying to force me to have sex with them. I had not even gone through puberty yet, and I knew that only married ladies had sex with their husbands. That is what I understood. It did not make any sense to me. I knew there was something terribly wrong with me, and somehow, this had to be part of whatever that was.

I made it through fifth grade, and the winter I was in sixth grade, a wonderful thing happened to me—I learned how to snow ski. There was a program at my brother's school where the kids could rent skis, boots, and poles, and a bus would pick them up at the school on Saturday and take them to the ski hill that was ninety minutes away, where they could then take ski lessons. My brother had been in the program for a year, and of course, I begged and begged to get to go with him. When I got into the sixth grade, I was finally allowed to take ski lessons. We both loved skiing. My brother was much more aggressive than I was and soon was jumping off moguls, going faster, and even doing flips.

Eventually our uncle, our mother's brother, started skiing and brought our aunt and both their kids along, and we had the whole family on the slopes. I loved my little cousins so much. We would play follow-the-leader coming down the main slope, and people could see us from the lodge at the base of the mountain. We would all be lined up across the hill, swishing and turning like a big snake. There was my uncle, my aunt, my brother, my two cousins, and any friends who tagged along. Sometimes our grandmother would come up to the lodge and watch us ski all day long.

When I started seventh grade, I got to go to the same school as my big brother! The high school was crowded, so they kept the freshmen at the junior high school with the seventh and eighth grades. I really did not see him very much because we were in different grades and different classes. I'd see him sometimes at lunch, and he would nod his head at me or give me a quick little wave. I was growing up and becoming a shapely young woman.

At first, I was thrilled to be in junior high, but I learned fast that life as a young teenager isn't always sweet or kind. The first week of school, I endured an embarrassing event in front of the whole class. It was still warm autumn days, so I had dressed in a plaid Scottish kilt with a white blouse and knee socks. It was a cute outfit. We were taking a quiz and were supposed to bring it up to the teacher's desk when we were done. I was sitting in the back of the room and had to walk between two rows of kids to get to the front with my quiz.

One of the boys from the football team was sitting at the front desk of that row, and when I passed him, he reached over and pulled down one of my knee socks. That wasn't so bad, but then he laughed out loud and pointed at my leg and said, "Look at all the hair on her legs!"

Of course, everyone in the room laughed. All I could do was pull my sock back up and sit down. I had asked my grandmother if I could shave my legs when I started junior high because we were allowed to wear nylons (pantyhose didn't come out until I was in high school). She would not allow me to shave my legs or wear any kind of makeup. All the girls wore eye shadows, mascara, and lipstick. I hadn't ever been interested in makeup because I was a skier. If you fall and plant your face in the snow, you'd come up a mess, and I certainly didn't want to be called "a ski bunny," which was a girl who worried more about what her hair and makeup looked like than she did skiing. I wasn't about to waste my time with that stuff. But not being able to shave my legs was embarrassing. I never told my grandmother what happened at school or how self-conscious and humiliated I had been. I just shaved my legs and never said anything.

There were always other kids I'd seen skiing on the hill who would talk to me at school. We'd sit together on the ski bus going home and talk about the teachers or our classes. It was a wonderful time for me. The kids who were in our neighborhood didn't ski, so we became part of another world with the kids who skied.

My big brother was becoming an incredibly good skier. He talked about joining the ski team when he got to high school and would begin racing. He was so comfortable on a pair of skis that he began doing silly tricks. There was a lift called the T-bar that went to the top of the mountain. You had to lean on a bar that pulled you up the hill. You couldn't sit on the bar because it would extend all the way to the ground, and you'd get jerked off and would have to ski down and start all over again. It could pull two people together up the hill. If you rode with my big brother, he'd do crazy things like reach down and unclip buckles on your ski boots, or he'd lift one of his skis up and cross it over his other ski and act like nothing was wrong.

It was a long ride, so we would strap our ski poles together and toss them across our boots so we wouldn't have to hassle with them until we got to the top of the mountain. Sometimes he'd reach down and toss my poles off to the side of the lift. I either had to jump off and grab them and ski down from there or leave them and ski from the top down without poles until I could find them. He was a big tease and thought it was all so funny.

One of his favorite tricks was to pick up his ski and put it between mine and then giggle at me trying to remain standing up. He was taller and heavier than me and could easily control the

T-bar. Nobody else tried those kinds of high jinks because they'd get reported to the ski patrol and could get kicked off the hill. I loved my big brother and enjoyed his teasing. If I got tired of his antics, I'd go ski on another hill so I wouldn't have to ride the T-bar with him. They eventually replaced that old T-bar with a chairlift.

Later that year, our uncle, our mother's brother, was killed in an airplane accident. This was a significant event for my brother. As I said, we went on vacations together and spent every birthday and every holiday either at their house or ours. My uncle was quite an outdoorsman. He didn't just hunt deer or elk; he hunted for the biggest deer and elk with antlers that might get him listed in the world records of the Boone and Crocket Club.

And he didn't just fish; he tied his own flies and fished for the biggest fish ever. He caught a trout that was so big, he kept it in his freezer for years. He took my brother hunting and fishing; he taught him how to tie flies and which ones to use. He taught my brother how to hunt, how to shoot, and how to dress out an animal. They talked about football all the time. They had become very close. He had been going hunting when the small private plane they were in crashed and killed the pilot and my uncle.

When my grandmother was told her son had been killed, she lost her mind for a while. It was no secret that she favored him over our mother. He had been the golden boy, the smartest, the best hunter, the best fisherman, had a beautiful wife and two adorable children, and successful at his job at the Federal Aviation Administration. When he was born, he had some medical problems and almost died. My grandmother must have spent many hours nursing him to health and may have forgotten that she had a three-year-old daughter at home who needed attention too. I believe this was the beginning of the conflict between my mother and grandmother that lasted their entire lives.

My mother, unlike her brother, had dropped out of high school and gotten married, had two kids while she was still a teenager, then gotten divorced and taken off. She dumped her kids on her parents without any notice and disappeared; that didn't help things between them.

Later, when I was an adult, she told me she spent that summer with one of her rich girlfriends who had a white Cadillac convertible. They went from town to town all summer, attending the rodeos across the state. There was a rodeo every weekend from May to September, and they brought with them the raucous, brawling parties for the cowboys and the women who were looking for a good time. My mother slept her way from rodeo to rodeo and finally hooked up with a cowboy who wasn't really competing anymore, but he looked good in tight jeans and fancy boots and paid for drinks and hotels.

When we were on our way from my uncle's funeral to the cemetery, I looked over at my big brother on the other side of the limousine. He had been quiet and kept to himself all week after we heard about the accident. He was staring out the window at nothing, and I watched one solitary tear run down his face. I had never seen him cry before, and it broke my heart that I couldn't take this pain from him.

Our grandmother was beyond heartbroken; she was inconsolable. She would drive out to the cemetery every morning before going to work at the hospital and spend an hour draped across the headstone and the grave, crying. She was there in sleet, snow, pouring rain, and hundred-degree weather for over a year, so she wasn't available to her two teenage grandchildren who needed her.

Our grandfather was a large tall man with huge hands. He was soft-spoken and rarely ever raised his voice. He was a kind gentleman who allowed our grandmother to do whatever she wanted to do. He worked his entire life at the same job from the time he quit high school when WWII started until he retired. He was too young to enlist, so he went to work at the smelter, where he became an electrician. He retired from that same job over forty years later.

He had married my grandmother after her first husband had died while working at the same smelter. He legally adopted my mother and uncle and raised them. Then he took my brother and me into his home and raised us; he never had any children of his own. I don't think he knew what to do about how my grandmother was behaving after we buried my uncle. She cried all the time, and you couldn't even talk to her, or she'd start crying and run into another room. He wasn't really a father figure for us because he was our grandfather. He didn't know how to help two teenagers with all the confusing things we were struggling with, so my brother and I had to figure out how to grieve on our own.

We had lost our father, and now the man who stepped in and became as close as a father to us was gone. How does a thirteen-year-old girl express to an adult that they desperately needed help? How does she explain that she believed that whatever was terribly wrong with her must have surely been the cause of this terrible thing that had happened to her family? I thought it was my fault, and if I had told somebody about this terrible thing that was wrong with me, that had caused my mommy to abandon me and caused my father to abandon me and now caused my uncle to be killed, it wouldn't have happened. That's a heavy burden for a child to believe.

My big brother struggled for a while. It seemed like nothing mattered to him anymore. But when the snow fell and skiing season started, our aunt offered to continue to drive us and some of our friends up to the mountain to ski that winter. Our grandparents bought us both brand-new skis, boots, and poles for Christmas and brand-new pale-blue ski parkas. I got a brand-new one-piece ski suit that was a beautiful rich-chocolate with pale-blue stripes that ran down each side. My brother got brand-new ski pants and sweaters to match. We got some money for Christmas that we spent on matching ski caps and new ski gloves. It sure made us feel special.

Then the inevitable happened—my brother became a sophomore and started attending high school, and I was in the eighth grade still at junior high. I didn't like being separated again, but things weren't as drastic this time. I had gotten involved in several of the art classes and assisted the teachers in creating bulletin boards that were in the many hallways at school. I enjoyed making colorful scenes for historical events or holidays, and there was always a dance coming up that we made posters for.

My grandmother did not allow me to date yet, but I could go to the dances, which were in the school's gymnasium, with a group of girlfriends. We only lived a block and a half away, so she would show up at the end of the dance and walk us home or drive us in the snowy weather.

I had always loved dancing and even wanted to be a ballet dancer when I was little. They played records of all the current popular songs, and I'd get asked to dance every dance. I had developed into a very shapely young woman and come to realize that was what was making me so popular with the boys. It was the '60s and rock and roll music was being played at all the dances. I could shimmy and shake and twist for three hours and have a ball.

It was also the age of miniskirts and hot pants, which I wasn't allowed to wear, so I had to be creative. I'd roll up the top of my skirt once I got to the dance, so it was shorter. And once I got to the gym, I'd take off the bulky sweater my grandmother made me wear and dance in the silky shirt I had on underneath the sweater. When I became a freshman, I was allowed to walk to the dances with my friends, but I still was not allowed to date. Most of the time, my grandmother sent my big brother over to make sure I got home safely after the dance. He had his driver's license by then, and I loved it when he'd come to pick me up. Those dances were some of the best times of my teenage life.

On the other side of being abandoned by my mother and father, I was certain that there was something terribly wrong with me. This caused me to be frightened to be alone and to be frightened and confused when my big brother got to do things without me. I would struggle with self-esteem as I grew into a young lady. I needed a strong father figure to help shape my understanding of the world and how it works. I needed a loving and understanding mother figure to help shape my morals and know how I was supposed to act as I grew up. What I had was a stressed grandmother, a loving grandfather, but nobody I could go to with questions about what I was feeling and what was happening to me.

CHAPTER 2

Our grandparents had both worked so long at their jobs that they each had a month of vacation every year. We spent many summers in the mountains fishing, hiking, or on one of the many lakes in the state. My grandmother grew up in a mining town that was booming with silver and gold mines. Her father was a supervisor of one of the mines, which was in a valley between the beautiful mountain ranges of the Rocky Mountains, so she loved going to the mountains to take us fishing, hiking, hunting, or camping.

My big brother taught me how to fish and how to shoot a rifle for hunting. The rule was if I wanted to fish, I had to put the live bait on the hook myself. When I got tired of the squiggly worms or the grasshoppers he used, he taught me how to fly-fish, and I learned how to tie my own flies. We would get up while it was still dark and take a car full of his buddies, and we'd go fishing all day long. Again, the rule was if you catch it, you clean it, and you eat it.

The older I got, the more fun it was to just tag along with all his buddies. The older I got, his buddies began to take notice that I had developed into a shapely female. Of course, I would take along my swimsuit and get into the creek and get cooled off. I remember one time I stumbled upon my big brother trying to catch a large trout in the shadows along the creek. I came splashing and giggling right into his fishing hole and scared the trout back down the stream. He was so frustrated, he threw his fishing pole onto the ground and stomped off. I didn't do it on purpose, but I should have known he was close and been a little more careful.

I was always playing in the water. I enjoyed that more than fishing. I'd get bored waiting for a fish to bite, and I didn't really have the patience to stand and wait. There were so many other wonderful things to do—walk through a beautiful mountain meadow, look for deer, watch out for bears or rattlesnakes, look for agates and pretty rocks, just sit in the sunshine and enjoy the fresh air, go for a swim, splash in the creek, jump off logs, and pretend that there really wasn't anything terribly wrong with me.

When my brother started driving, that added a whole new dimension to our skiing. He always wanted to be the first person down the hill, so we took off very early. We packed our lunches the night before, so all we had to do was get dressed and go. When I was a freshman, my grandmother still would not allow me to go out on dates alone with one guy. But if my brother went and we all went together with a group of kids, she was okay with that.

In the summer, on Friday nights, we'd either go swimming at the college pool or to one of the drive-in theaters in town. My brother would take his girlfriend and two or three buddies and me. He told me once he wasn't going to bring anymore of his friends home because all they wanted to do was spend time with me. It became a joke between us.

There was one incident one summer that proved the point— that I was all grown up and had quite a body. A young actress was featured in *Playboy* magazine, and all the guys were drooling over the pictures. The magazine listed her measurements, and when I saw what they were, I laughed out loud and said my measurements were better than hers. Of course, the guys didn't believe me and started making snide comments. I offered to prove it to them and went and put on my two-piece bikini and brought them a tape measure. My bust was an inch larger, my waist was two inches smaller, and my hips were an inch larger than hers. That shut them up, and I had several dates for the following weekends.

When I finally became a sophomore and would be attending the same school as my big brother again, I was thrilled. I was so proud of him that I told everyone I met that I had a big brother who was a senior. I was so excited when one of my teachers asked me if I was related to him and I could say, "Yes, I am! He's my big brother!"

We had grown so close over the years, and we had always looked out for each other. There was a particularly nasty junior in one of my art classes who began teasing me. He'd walk by and slam my locker or pull my hair or push my books off the desk onto the floor. He was also a skier, and we had seen him and his older brother on the hill before.

One day, he asked me if I could help get some props from the storage room behind the stage. We were both in a class called stage-craft; we built the sets and ran the lighting for the various shows and plays that the high school put on each year. I went with him, and when we got up to the old room, he pushed me in and stepped out and locked the door. I knew he was just pulling hijinks again and didn't think too much about it. I figured he'd let me out before I was late to the next class.

When I heard the bell ring, I got a little more worried. The storage room was behind the stage. There weren't any classrooms close, so even if I yelled nobody was going to hear me. I didn't think he was going to make me stay there all night, but I was getting angry and trying to figure out what I was going to tell the teacher about why I wasn't in class. After what seemed like hours, he finally came and unlocked the door. He said the teacher wanted to see me. I went right down to class and figured something had been said when the teacher called roll.

I told my big brother that night what had happened and asked him if he could teach me how to hit this guy in the mouth. I'd had enough of his irritating and stupid behavior. My brother showed me how to stand, then he showed me how to make a fist, then we practiced hitting each other until we were both sore. He told me not to worry about the guy, that he'd take care of it. He said I needed a lot more practice to be able to protect myself anyway.

A couple days later, I saw the guy, and he had a black eye. He told everybody he got hit in football practice. He wasn't on the football team. He never bothered me again.

As a sophomore in high school, I began to believe that whatever it was that was so wrong with me had gone away, or at least people couldn't see it anymore. My grandmother allowed me to begin dating, and there were always a lot of guys hanging around me. I was astounded that they couldn't see whatever it was that had been so terribly wrong with me. I began to gain a little confidence and hoped that things would get better.

One guy I particularly liked asked me to go to the movies. He owned a motorcycle and told me that's what he'd be picking me up with, so I needed to be sure to not wear a skirt. I wore jeans and brought a jeans jacket. I loved being back on a motorcycle and was thrilled when he offered to take me for an all-day ride the next weekend. I had long hair that reached down to my fanny, so when I wore the helmet he brought me, it flowed out behind us in the wind. Sometimes I'd tuck it all up into the helmet, and when we'd stop somewhere, I'd take the helmet off, and all that hair would come falling down and blowing in the breeze. We enjoyed riding together that summer.

It was the next fall when our mother arrived back in town and moved in with us at our grandparents' home. Her husband had beaten her again, and she'd been in the hospital. When she was released, she packed her things and came home. She'd had an adorable little poodle that her husband had grabbed in a drunken rage and broken its neck right in front of her.

She got a job and eventually rented a two-bedroom trailer. She asked me if I wanted to come and live with her. I thought it might be better than the stifling attitude my grandmother had been giving me, so I moved my clothes to my mother's trailer. When my boyfriend with the motorcycle came to pick me up for our date that weekend, she started to tell me what time I'd have to be home. I looked at her and said, "Who do you think you are? My mother? I'll be home when I get here. Don't wait up."

I didn't much like my mother. In fact, I hated her. She walked out and dumped me at her parents' and took off to sleep her way from cowboy to cowboy. She preferred her violent husband for years over having a decent life or taking care of her two children. I agreed to live with her to get some freedom, so I wasn't about to tolerate her trying to act like she was a mother.

The young man with the motorcycle got serious and asked me to marry him. I adored him and loved being with him, but I wasn't ready to get married. We remained friends through high school, and he'd come by and take me for bike rides occasionally.

I had been dating one of my brother's best friends, and we hung around together as a group. He also skied, so we went from summer into winter easily. My mother didn't like him, and she paid one of my brother's other buddies to take me out. She gave him money to buy some booze and told him to get me drunk and have his way with me. She was betting when she told the other guy that I'd been unfaithful to him, he'd just take off.

It didn't quite happen the way she planned. He bought the booze, some kind of cheap wine that I didn't much like, so I didn't drink enough to get drunk. He never got to first base. We started remembering silly things we'd all done over the years, and we laughed, giggled, and had a good time. I didn't think anything of being with any of my brother's friends because that's how it had always been. We'd all hung around with each other for so many years, they were all like my brothers.

They didn't all feel like that toward me. When I started dating them, making out, and so on, things changed. I started to really like one of the guys and spent more time with him than any of the others. He was a great skier and incredibly good-looking. I fell into my first huge crush. When we went on a date, I got so nervous. I changed clothes several times and just couldn't decide what to wear. I was a little surprised that he finally asked me out, and I wanted to do everything right. I wanted to be as pretty as I could, and I wanted to be a little sexy, and I just wanted him to like me as much as I liked him. He was on the ski team with my brother, so he was out of town for ski races most weekends. We went out whenever he was home again.

I never knew what happened. He just started not showing up, he quit calling me, and he'd go out of his way to not run into me at school. I guessed that he had figured out what it was that was so terribly wrong with me and was no longer interested.

Another one of my brother's friends, who was a skier and a senior, was interested in taking me out. I accepted the next time he asked. We had a great time. He treated me like I was special. He'd bring me a rose for no reason. He complimented me on whatever I was wearing. He planned on getting a degree in geology, and we'd go off into the mountains and look for gold. He enjoyed being in the mountains as much as I did. We were good together. He was over six feet tall, which was important because I wasn't a petite girl. I was five feet seven inches tall and was slender and voluptuous. I was certain that whatever it was that was terribly wrong with me, he couldn't see it. I enjoyed being with him.

Then they all graduated—my brother and all the group that we skied with. I was the only one who wasn't a senior. I was so proud of my big brother and excited for everyone to take the next steps of their lives. My boyfriend and I had talked about getting married after I graduated, so we told everyone that we were engaged. It was 1970, and the Vietnam War was going on. There was still the military draft, and if the men didn't get a college deferment, they could be drafted.

My boyfriend decided that he was going to enlist so he could choose which service he wanted. He knew karate and had always talked about becoming a Green Beret in the Special Forces. That way, the military would pay for his college to get the geology degree. He went to boot camp and was faithful to write and call when he could.

It was hard to have him gone. I did what I always did—hang out with my big brother and all his buddies. They all knew I was engaged, so there was no more dating. I'd go to the state fair with four or five guys; we'd go fishing all day, swimming at the college pool, and hunting the next fall. We'd go to movies and catch some of the rodeos. That fall, my brother went away to college, and I was alone again.

On the other side of puberty was confusion for me. I heard my brother and his friends talking about the sexy girls at school and tried to emulate what they did, how they dressed and wore their hair. The line between being "a good girl" and being something else was difficult for me. I didn't know how to be a good girl and be sexy so the boys would like me. It seemed like the more I developed a curvy body, my clothes became less "sweet and nice" and became tighter and revealing. Wasn't that what they wanted? Wasn't that what girls were supposed to do?

After I went through puberty, my grandmother pulled away from me. She started telling me that I was just like my mother, and she wasn't saying it in a nice way. I knew I looked a lot like my mother; we had similar facial features, but I didn't think I was a selfish, self-centered person at all. I have always tried to be helpful and kind. How could I be anything close to her? I just wanted the boys to like me and to not see whatever it was that was wrong with me. I worked hard to make that happen.

CHAPTER 3

My fiancé came home on leave for a week after boot camp, and I couldn't have been prouder. He was required to wear his military uniform when he traveled, and he looked so incredible when I picked him up at the airport. My mother was exceptionally proud and bragged to all the women she worked with about her handsome soon-to-be-son-in-law.

That first night, he told me to dress up because he was taking me to the finest restaurant in town for dinner. He had a table reserved, special wine ordered, and there were beautiful candles on the table and a bouquet of flowers for me. It was so romantic. The drinking age had been lowered to eighteen because the boys they were drafting and sending to Vietnam were eighteen. They felt if they were old enough to fight for their country, they should be able to have a beer. My fiancé was over nineteen, and I had always looked older than I really was. When I was sixteen and seventeen, I looked twenty or twenty-one. I never got carded when we'd all go to the bars to dance.

He was sweet and attentive while he was home, but his parents also wanted to spend some time with him, so we spent a few evenings apart. The time went so fast. The last night he was home, we went to see the movie *Love Story*, starring Ryan O'Neal and Ali MacGraw. It was a sad story about two people who fall in love, get married, and then she dies. I was very emotional after watching it, and we went to a beautiful park and sat in the moonlight and talked.

He held me close and kissed me so tenderly. When he said, "Did you know you have the most beautiful eyes I've ever seen?"

I was breathless. Then he said, "You know, when I get back to the base, it is likely that I will be sent to Vietnam." We hadn't really talked about what was happening next with his assignment. I became alarmed. He cuddled me and rocked me back and forth and spoke so softly while he was kissing my neck. When he asked if I wanted to make love with him, it didn't take me long to agree. I gave him all my love, knowing that we were going to be married and would live happily ever after.

Two months later, I realized that I was pregnant. My grand-mother stopped speaking to me, so she wasn't any help. My big brother was busy getting ready for college. I told my mother that we were going to be married anyway, so it wasn't a big deal, but she decided to take matters into her own hands. She made an appoint-ment with the OB-GYN doctor to have a pregnancy test. When we got there, she went into the exam room first. She was in there for over an hour. A nurse came and got me and had me pee in a cup; she told me I was pregnant and sent me back to the waiting room. I never saw the doctor. When my mother came out, we left. She told me the doctor would schedule an abortion for the next week, and that would take care of my problem. I wasn't sure what an abortion was, and I didn't think I had a problem.

I had called my fiancé and left a message for him to please call me as soon as he could. When he called that evening, my mother took the phone from me and spoke to him first. She told him I was pregnant. Then she told him that I was too young to get married and needed to finish high school first. He asked to talk to me, so she gave me the phone. He asked if I was okay, and I said I just wanted things to be all right and that I wanted to be married and have this baby with him. He said all the things I wanted to hear, that we would get married, and everything would be fine.

My mother grabbed the phone away from me and screamed at him that if I didn't go have the abortion, she would file charges of statutory rape against him. He could be dishonorably discharged and go to jail. It would ruin his military career and destroy his chances to go to college.

I couldn't believe what she was saying. I told her he never raped me and that I had wanted to make love with him. She told us because I was sixteen, it didn't matter that I consented. That's why it's called statutory rape. I knew she'd do it and told him. I didn't want to be the reason his career was destroyed. He told me it was my choice.

It really wasn't my choice at all. I was naive and uneducated about all of this, and I was manipulated by a mother who wasn't going to allow me to make the same mistakes she had made. She told me years later that she had told the doctor if he didn't perform the abortion on me, she would call his wife and tell her that they were having an affair. She said she'd tell the television and news people and that it would ruin his practice. Abortion was illegal at that time; it was before the Supreme Court's *Roe v. Wade* decision.

Abortions were only legal if it was necessary to save the mother's life. I was perfectly healthy, strong, and would have been able to carry that baby to term just fine. There was no risk to my life. The doctor agreed to do an illegal abortion because my mother threatened him, and he believed she would ruin his life. I agreed to have the illegal abortion because I believed that she would ruin my fiancé's life.

Growing up with my grandmother, a registered nurse in the newborn nursery at the hospital, meant that we knew all the doctors and most of the nurses she worked with and were comfortable going in and out of the hospital. My brother and I had our share of broken bones, torn ligaments, and visits to the emergency room, so I felt comfortable about having this procedure. Being in the hospital was like a second home to me. My brother and I had walked or ridden our bikes to have lunch with our grandmother at the hospital for years. We knew the back hallways, the secret passages, and all the ways in and out of the place. All the doctors who knew my grandmother seemed to adore and respect her. Some of them had even made house calls when we had gotten sick. They were more like friends to us. I wasn't afraid to go to the hospital and believed the doctor would treat me like they all had before.

My mother took me to the hospital that morning and got me checked in. A nurse took me to my room, and my mother went to work. I was left alone. The nurse came back and told me to get undressed and put on a gown she had lain on the bed. After a while, a nurse aide came to the room with a gurney and had me lie down on it while she pushed me to the operating room. She covered me with a heated blanket. I was a little nervous, but the blanket helped me relax.

My appendix ruptured the summer before, and I was rushed into the same operating room to save my life. I remember before that surgery that they gave me something to go to sleep. I thought they would be doing that as soon as I got to the operating room. That didn't happen. When they pushed me into the operating room, the doctor yelled at the nurses to get me up onto the table. I was pulling the gown around me, and the doctor yelled for the nurse to remove the gown and take it away. I was lying on the cold metal operating table completely naked. There were several nurses in the room, and one wall was all glass, and there were people standing there, watching what was going on.

One of the nurses brought over a warmed blanket and began to wrap it around me. The doctor yelled for her to remove it. I began to feel scared and started to tremble. Something wasn't right. I had never heard a doctor yell like that before. I asked if they were going to give me something to go to sleep. A nurse started toward me with a small white cup with a pill in it, but the doctor told her to take it back. He looked at me and said something like, "You were awake when you got yourself into this, so you can just stay awake while I clean up your mess."

The doctor told me to put my legs up in the stirrups. I had never seen stirrups before and didn't like putting my legs up in the air while I was stark naked. The nurses carefully guided my legs into the stirrups and strapped them in. I couldn't move. When they strapped my arms to the sides of the operating table, I became very frightened. The doctor shoved something cold and metal into my vagina. I had never even had a pelvic exam before, so this was terrifying to me. The doctor picked up a spoon-shaped instrument that looked like a double-sided knife. When he shoved it into me, it hurt so bad that I let out a yelp. The doctor asked me if I liked it and shoved the knife back into me again. He kept shoving it in so hard that I began to cry.

He'd pull it out and sling bloody tissue across the floor. I didn't know that he was killing my unborn child. My mother told me that she'd had several abortions and that there really wasn't a baby there yet. She told me all it was when you were first pregnant was a blob of tissue. I was in my fourth month; I didn't know what to think.

The nurses stood back and seemed stunned at how the doctor was treating me. He would lean in between my legs and glare at me and ask, "Is this how you like it?"

I didn't understand. What was I supposed to like? Being stabbed and sliced to pieces and having to lie there, strapped down to that cold metal table with my naked legs spread open in front of him? Was I supposed to enjoy being forced to lie there naked in front of everyone while he yelled at me?

I was trembling and started crying even harder. I was always the tough little girl hanging out with my big brother and his buddies, so I told myself I had to be tough now. I gritted my teeth and waited for the next assault. He cruelly shoved that instrument into me and sliced and cut everything out with harsh, mean strokes. I was sobbing so hard that one of the nurses came over and took my hand and quietly told me it would all be over soon.

Someone said something about my blood pressure, but the doctor ignored the nurses and kept stabbing me. I felt strange and tried to tell the nurse who was holding my hand. Then the oldest nurse in the room—I thought she was the head nurse stepped between me and the doctor and said very sternly, "She's going into shock. You need to stop this now."

The doctor looked like she'd slapped him. He threw the instrument across the room, and I saw my blood and tissue splatter on the floor. He turned abruptly and stormed out of the operating room, saying, "Fine. Clean up this mess."

One of the nurses immediately brought me a warmed blanket and covered me. Another one gave me a pill and told me it would help with the pain. Several of the nurses had unstrapped my legs and lifted the stirrups out so I could lie flat. They washed me with warm water and cleaned up the blood that had splattered all over my body.

It took a few minutes for me to stop crying. The nurse who had held my hand brought me a warm washcloth and wiped my face and neck. Then she offered me something cool to drink and said it would help. They dressed me in a clean gown and got me back onto a clean gurney with a soft pillow and warm blankets. I thanked them for their kindness. They seemed subdued and almost frightened. One of them patted my shoulder and said I should rest today and that I would be released tomorrow. Then one of them took me back to my room.

Every time any family member had to go to the hospital while I was growing up, we always went and visited them, brought them flowers or magazines to read. I was certain that my grandmother would stop by that afternoon when she got off her shift to see how I was doing. She never came. While I lay there waiting, I was in quite a bit of pain. The floor nurse told me she'd have to call the doctor to see if she could give me something. I didn't want her to do that, so I said I'd wait a while longer.

When my grandmother didn't show up, I called home to see if anything was wrong. My grandfather answered the phone. I told him I was waiting for her to stop by, but she hadn't, so I was worried. He told me she was home, but she didn't want to speak to me. I told him that something horrible had happened to me and that I was scared and wanted to talk to my grandmother about it. He asked her again if she would talk to me; she said no. I didn't know until many years later when we finally did discuss what happened that they posted the surgeries on a bulletin board in the hospital each day. When my name was on that list, people who knew who I was had come to ask her what was wrong and if I was okay. My grandmother was embarrassed and humiliated that her granddaughter had to have an abortion and that she had to tell everyone when they asked about me. She didn't know what the doctor had done to me, how he had treated me. I didn't know, and none of the nurses knew that my mother had threatened him to get him to do the abortion on me. I lay there in that hospital bed, thinking that my big brother might come to visit me, or my mother would certainly come after she got off work. I watched the sun set outside, and the hours passed slowly.

When nobody came to visit me, I began to understand. I knew that I had done the worst thing a girl could do. I had sex before I was married. That was what my grandmother had taught me. I tried to justify my actions because I was engaged to be married. Somehow, that didn't help me right then. Someone brought me a dinner tray. I didn't feel much like eating. I was sick to my stomach and in so much pain. I tried Jell-O and some mashed potatoes. The nurse tried to get me to eat more but finally just took the tray away.

She brought me another pill and said it would help me sleep. It didn't. I lay awake all night, thinking and crying. Every time a nurse would come in to check on me, I'd just roll over and face the wall. I didn't want to talk to anyone anymore. I felt so horribly alone. I guessed that the reason none of my family wanted to visit me or even find out if I was all right was because there really was something terribly wrong with me. I had thought I'd outgrown whatever it was, but lying there all alone in the dark proved I was wrong.

I listened while the nurses changed shifts early the next morning. I watched the doctors make their rounds, going from room to room. My doctor never came to my room. They brought me a breakfast tray that I enjoyed because I was hungry. Then one of the nurses told me I could take a shower and get dressed. I was still bleeding, so she brought me several pads to use. The shower felt so good.

After I had eaten and showered, the nurse told me I had to get up and leave because they needed the room for the next patient. I thought I'd be able to stay there until someone came to pick me up. They told me I couldn't do that, so I packed up my things and called my mother. She said she couldn't come get me until she got off work that evening. I told her they kicked me out of the room, and I didn't have anywhere to go. She told me to go sit in the lobby and wait for her there. It was just after ten in the morning. She didn't get off work until six in the evening.

I went to the lobby and sat and waited. The cafeteria was right next to the lobby, and around lunchtime, I could smell the food. I didn't have any money, so I wasn't able to get anything to eat. I walked down the hall to the water fountain and got a drink of water. Then I walked outside and around the hospital. I had to change the pad because I was still bleeding so much, so I went back into the bathroom. As I sat there in the lobby, watching people go up to visit their loved ones, something happened to me. I spent the entire day thinking about how my whole family had deserted me. I figured if I had already done the worst thing a girl could do—have sex before getting married—then it didn't matter what I did anymore.

Around 6:30 p.m., I saw my mother pull up to the front door of the hospital. I walked out and got into the car. I knew that I wasn't the same person who had walked into that place just the day before. I didn't feel well and went to bed when we got to her trailer. She fixed something for dinner, and after eating, I went back to bed. I didn't get up the next morning before she left for work. I decided that if it didn't matter anymore what I did, I could skip classes if I wanted to. I didn't have to do tons of homework; I didn't have to take part in any of the clubs or organizations that I had joined at school the year before. I just didn't care anymore.

My grandmother was refusing to speak to me. It was her way of demanding that if I didn't comply with her rules, she would withhold her love. She taught that lesson very well. My big brother must have been so disgusted with me. When he found out that I was pregnant, he had slapped my face. My fiancé was hundreds of miles away and had been very relieved when I told him I had chosen to have the abortion. I didn't know when I'd see him again. I never told any of my girlfriends at school. They never knew I was pregnant, so I decided not to tell them about the abortion. We were starting our junior year. They were all getting college applications and taking SAT tests. I didn't have any money, so there was no way I'd ever go to college.

Since I had already done the worst thing a girl could do, I decided to try things that I had never done before. I skipped class to go skiing that winter. I tried smoking cigarettes and found that I liked the menthol-flavored ones. If I was at a party and someone passed around a marijuana joint, I'd try it. As a skier, I had tried to stay in good physical condition, so I had never felt taking any kind of pills or drugs was smart. I didn't go that far. I knew that if I dressed a certain way, I'd get lots of attention from men. I stopped wearing the expensive ski outfits my grandmother had bought for me and wore my jeans and jean jacket to ski in. The jeans fit tightly, and the sweaters I wore showed off my curvy figure. I started wearing shorter skirts to school and tighter sweaters. I looked different and felt different. I knew that it didn't matter what I did. I could do whatever I wanted.

My fiancé wrote fewer letters and didn't call as much as I would have liked. I knew that he was going through some tough training, but I was feeling so shunned by everyone I loved that I assumed he didn't want to have anything to do with me either. That was until he got his next leave and came home for another week. The first thing he did was get a hotel room for us to be able to have sex again. That told me what I was good for. Every time I talked about getting married, he'd bring up that I still had another year until I would graduate from high school. That didn't mean we couldn't make love with each other now. I was so desperate for somebody to give a damn about me that the attention he gave me felt good, but I demanded that we use condoms so I wouldn't get pregnant again.

I don't remember much about my junior year in high school. I attended most of my classes and did most of the homework just because I enjoyed doing it. I'd hang out with different guys, telling them that I was engaged, but he was far away, and who knew when he would come back.

I realized that I could be in control. I could say whom I wanted to have sex with or not. I could choose. I was smart enough to know that having sex with men was giving myself to them. I knew they didn't love me. I didn't need them to love me. I needed them to pay attention to me. The more men I could get to pay attention to me, the less I felt there was something wrong with me.

Whenever my fiancé got leave and came home, we'd go out and have fun and then have sex. He was handsome, and he did pay attention to me when he was home, and I do believe that I loved him for a time, but I wasn't the same person as when he first met me. I didn't get to go to any of our homecoming dances because I had a fiancé, but he was always gone when the dances were held. I never went to any proms for the same reason. I think that began to make me feel like I was missing so much while I was waiting for him. Somehow, I made it through my senior year, but when I walked across the stage and got my diploma, I knew I was three months pregnant.

I had not told anyone, and no one knew. For some reason, I didn't have the terrible morning sickness that I'd had the first time, which was how my grandmother knew before I did. After graduating, I took a full-time job as a waitress in a classy new joint that summer. I saved my money. The next time my fiancé called me, I told him I was pregnant again, and he was either going to marry me this time, or he could pay for the abortion. I bought a cute little white dress to wear as a wedding dress and showed it to him the last time he had been in town. I told him I had saved enough money to fly to where he was. He told me to pack my wedding dress and come to him.

I quit my job, packed my things, and flew across the country. He met my plane and had arranged for us to live off base with another couple, sharing rent for a trailer house. I was not allowed on base because I wasn't his wife. I sat in the tiny bedroom and waited for him to arrive each evening. We all shared in house-cleaning duties, and we contributed to groceries, and we mostly ate meals together. There was little privacy, so we would go for a walk or ride into town.

After a few weeks, I began asking when we would be getting married. He gave me every reason for why we shouldn't get married. I saw the writing on the wall and said he had better find out where we could get an abortion. There were several states that were allowing first trimester abortions. That meant that you had to be within the first three months, or they wouldn't do the abortion. I was already five months pregnant by that time. He found a place in New York City, so he got a leave for a long weekend, and we rode a train from North Carolina to New York City. We stayed in an old hotel close to the railroad station.

That night, all I could think about was what was going to happen to me the next day, and I couldn't sleep. There was a claw-foot bathtub in the bathroom, so I got up and took a warm bath. I thought it would calm me down, but all I could think about was what happened the last time I'd had an abortion. It had been so traumatic for me, and I wasn't sure I could go through that again. I cried until the water became too cold to sit in any longer. I went back to bed and tried to get some sleep.

The next morning, we walked to the abortion facility. There was a whole room full of women waiting to have an abortion. When it was my turn, I was trembling and scared. A woman asked me how pregnant I was. I told her I thought I was about two and a half months. She told me that the doctor would come in and give me an examination, and then they would perform a suction abortion. She explained that they would put me to sleep and suck out the contents in my uterus with a powerful vacuum. She said it would take about twenty minutes, and then I'd be taken into the recovery room where I would wake up.

Knowing that they were going to put me to sleep helped me calm down. The doctor did the exam and asked me when my last period was. I told him two and a half months ago. I am certain that he knew I was more than two and a half months pregnant; any doctor would have known I was further along than that. I got scared that they might refuse to do the abortion, but someone came in and gave me a pill and told me it would help me go to sleep and said everything would be all done when I woke up. I still didn't realize that I was allowing them to kill my baby to solve my problem. I was so messed up and confused. I knew I was messed up, but I just didn't know what to do about it.

When I woke up, most of the other women had gotten dressed and gone home. I was in a lot of pain, and it took me some time to get up and get going. My fiancé was waiting for me when I was finally able to get dressed and leave. We had to get back to the base, so we went right to the train station and took the next train back to North Carolina. I was hemorrhaging badly and had to keep going to the restroom on the train to change pads. I was sick to my stomach, and the rocking of the train only made me feel worse.

When we got back to the trailer, it was late at night, so we had to be quiet and not wake the other couple up. When I woke the next morning, the men were already gone. I wandered out and told the other gal that I wasn't feeling well and was going to spend the day in bed. She offered to bring me a cup of tea, and I was grateful. I didn't know if she knew what had happened. I had never told them that I was pregnant. It felt like everything inside me was on fire. I was sweating and hot and going in and out of sleep for days. My fiancé bought some aspirin for me, and that seemed to help ease the pain a little bit.

I didn't seem to be getting better, and after two weeks, I was still bleeding heavily and was becoming weak. We couldn't make love, so my fiancé slept most nights on the base. He couldn't take me to the base doctor because I wasn't his wife. I was scared that there was something wrong, but I didn't have any money to pay for a doctor or go to an emergency room. My fiancé had used all his cash to pay for the train trip and the abortion.

I called my grandmother, who hadn't spoken to me for two years, and asked her if she would send me some money so I could come home. We both cried and said that we loved each other, and she paid for a plane ticket home. I packed my things, and my fiancé drove me to the airport. It was obvious that he was relieved about my going back home and not making a fuss about getting married. On the plane, I watched the clouds out the window and the ground going by below, and I said to myself, "There has got to be something more to life than having sex, getting pregnant, having an abortion, having sex, getting pregnant, and having an abortion." I didn't know what it might be or how I might find it, but I decided this wasn't what I wanted my life to be anymore.

My grandmother picked me up at the airport and took me to her house. It was Thanksgiving Day, and my whole family was there. I had never told them that I had been pregnant again or that I'd had another abortion. No one ever asked me about being gone or what I did or what had happened. They did ask about my fiancé. I didn't talk about him too much after I got back home. He didn't call as often as he used to, and he didn't write as many letters as he had before. I stayed with my mother and spent some time just trying to feel better.

On the other side of having a second illegal abortion was just pain. My grandmother took me to see a doctor. and I was taking medication for an infection, but the pain was deeper than an infection. Something inside of me was broken. I knew that there was always something terribly wrong with me, and I was certain that I could figure out what it was. I would do whatever I could to fix it, but I was so sick and exhausted. All I could manage was to get up each morning and take a shower and go back to bed. I wanted the pain of being alone to stop. I wanted the pain of being used to stop. I wanted the pain of being confused and unsure of what I was supposed to do to stop. I wanted the pain of waiting for my fiancé to be here so we could be together to stop. But I knew when he took me to the airport and put me on that plane that we weren't going to ever get married.

There had to be something more to life, and I wanted to discover what it was. I was eighteen years old, had been pregnant twice, had two illegal abortions, had a fiancé who was across the country and might be sent to Vietnam and never come back. I had my high school diploma but no job. That was where I needed to start. I sent off applications to several of the ski resorts around the state and waited to hear back from them. I decided what I needed was a job and to ski. Skiing always gave me exhilaration, contentment, total wonderment and awe at the beauty and majesty of the mountains and the snow, and it always gave me a sense of confidence. I waited anxiously to hear back from the resorts.

CHAPTER 4

There was so much inside of me that was confused. I heard from one of the ski resorts and had been told I got the job, but there wasn't enough snow yet, so I had to wait a couple weeks before starting. I was feeling better every day, and with the prospect of working at the ski resort so I could ski all winter, I felt like things in my life were getting better.

I rented a room at one of the town's oldest and best-known vintage hotels. There wasn't even a bathroom in my room. I had to go down the hall to shower and use the bathroom, but it was extremely cheap, clean, and I felt safer than if I'd tried to rent an apartment or a cabin. There were people all around me. I wouldn't really be alone. That appealed to me, so I moved my clothes and things into the beautiful antique-filled hotel room that was right on the corner of the road that led up to the ski resort where I would be working as a waitress.

The next few weeks were busy. It snowed every day, so ski conditions for the Christmas week were fantastic. The resort was fully booked. I worked hard every morning and found out I was good at waitressing. I made terrific tips, and several groups even requested to sit at my tables. When someone recognized me skiing in the afternoons, I would get invitations to ski with them. The resort had a heated outdoor swimming pool and indoor saunas. We were allowed to eat in the dining room if we were off shift, so it saved me a lot of money to have dinner there. I worked until lunch was set up, skied until it got dark, had dinner, then I'd usually swim laps in the pool. It was incredible to swim in the warm water and watch the snowflakes drift down to the pool. I'd get back to my hotel and fall into bed and sleep like a baby. I was getting into the best shape, and it felt good.

January came with horrible storms, but that was good for snow depth and skiing. It brought more guests and filled the hotel rooms. Someone said a guest was asking if anyone wanted to babysit for them while they went to the bar for a few hours. Many families came with children and stayed for a week at a time. I was off the next day anyway, so I said I'd do it. It was extra bucks in my pocket. The kids were fun, and I enjoyed being with them. It got around to the other hotels on the mountain that there was someone available to do babysitting. After my shift and skiing in the afternoon, I made good money for the next month just playing with kids.

But it cost me. One of the little buggers was sick with a bad cold and I caught it. When it turned so bad that my temperature got to 102 degrees, I went to the doctor. I was diagnosed with pneumonia and told to take a few days off and rest. I was given a prescription for the cough, Tylenol for the fever and aches, and I went back to my hotel to rest. I stopped at the grocery store and bought a bunch of microwaveable dinners, some microwaveable oatmeal, some soups, and a lot of 7Up to drink. I called my boss and explained, and he told me to take the whole week off. It was a good thing I'd made all that extra money babysitting all month long.

I was so sick for several days. All I did was take medicine and sleep. When I could get up, I took a hot shower and got dressed. When I came back to my room, I felt good enough to clean up the mess that I'd been making. I bagged up the empty food containers and piles of used Kleenex and took it all down to the trash room. I asked for clean sheets and towels. I found two books that had been given to me, so I cuddled up on my freshly made bed with a hot cup of tea and settled down to read.

Both books were written by Rev. Merlin Carothers, who had been an army chaplain. The first book I read was *Prison to Praise*. It was Reverend Carothers's own story of him getting through World War II in the army. It wasn't about a prison facility; it was about a prison of choices, situations, and consequences. He went from being a bitter, unhappy man to accepting Jesus and became born-again. I'd heard that phrase before but wasn't sure what it meant. I'd heard it on a Billy Graham program, and I wanted to know more and kept reading.

On the other side of thinking I was in love with a fiancé who was never there and might even be sent to Vietnam and might never come back was a very lonely, confused young woman. I desperately just wanted to be loved.

CHAPTER 5

Two days later, I was face down on the floor of my room, sobbing. I had finished both books. The second book was *Power in Praise* and continued Reverend Carothers's story. I carefully read the scriptures he quoted from his Bible.

There was a Bible in my hotel room, and I found that it had a table of contents of all the names of the books, which made it easier for me to find the scriptures he quoted. I kept going back to one specific scripture that I was sure I had heard somewhere before. It was in the New Testament and says, "For God so loved the world that he gave his only Son, that whoever believes in him will not perish but will have eternal life" (John 3:16). Reverend Carothers talked about how God created people to have fellowship with him, but God also gave us free will. That means that we get to choose for ourselves. People became stubborn and grew more independent until fellowship with God was broken. This self-will or rebellion is what the Bible calls sin.

Another scripture was in the book of Romans: "All have sinned and fallen short of the glory of God" (3:23). I never thought about the choices I had made as being a sin or not, but that scripture made it clear that all people (you, me—all people) have sinned. Romans 6:23 says, "The wages of sin is death, but the gift of God is eternal life." I knew all the people were going to die, but it did not make sense to me until I went back to John 3:16 again. God so loved the world—and me—that he sent his Son, Jesus, to earth to save us— and me—and if we believe in Jesus, we will not perish but will have eternal life. The payment for our sins was Jesus's life. He died for my sins. He died for your sins. Instead of me having to pay for my sins, Jesus has already paid for them in my place. God shows us that he loves us because while we were still sinners, Jesus died for us (Romans 5:8).

I read further in the book of John; he was one of the original disciples Jesus chose. Jesus was teaching the disciples about heaven and said, "You know the way to the place where I am going."

Thomas was confused and asked Jesus, "Lord, we don't know where you are going, so how can we know the way?"

In John 14:6, Jesus answered him, saying, "I am the way, the truth, and the life. No one comes to the father except through me."

I was beginning to understand. God created people and loves us and wants to have fellowship with us. Because I am a sinner, I have become separated from God and cannot experience that fellowship unless I became saved. How could I be saved? Reverend Carothers said being saved was being born again. In John 3:3, Jesus plainly says, "I tell you the truth, unless a man [or woman] is born again he [or she] cannot see the kingdom of God." There it was!

But how does someone be born again? Reverend Carothers said we must individually ask Jesus to be our personal Savior. I had gone to Catholic church and knew that Jesus was the Son of God and that he died on the cross to save the world from our sins. That was not enough. I had to receive Jesus by first turning to God and admitting I had committed sins, regretting what I had done. Then I asked Jesus to come into my life and forgive my sins so that I would be born again. Christ said in Revelation 3:20, "Behold, I stand at the door and knock; if anyone hears my voice and opens the door, I will come into him."

I got down on the floor of that little hotel room and got on my knees. I wasn't sure how to pray, but I was humbled by the thought that God was truly listening to me. I just started by telling him I had committed some terrible sins, and I told him everything I could remember. I said I was so sorry and truly regretted making the choices I'd made. I told him I wanted to do better, but I needed his help. I said I wanted to be born again and that I wanted Jesus to be my Savior. I thanked Jesus for dying on the cross to pay for my sins, but I didn't think that Jesus could love somebody like me, somebody who had committed the sins that I had.

Suddenly, the room disappeared. I was standing in the dirt on a hill. I could see Jesus hanging on the cross. I saw how his face had been beaten; his back had been whipped and was bleeding. There was a crown of thorns shoved into his head, and blood was streaming down his face. I saw the nails pounded through his hands and his feet. I could smell the stench of blood and sweat. I could hear women behind me weeping. I saw Roman guards standing off to the side, talking. I didn't understand what they were saying. I became aware of the oppressive heat and could feel sweat running down my back.

And then Jesus raised his head and looked right at me. I knew that he was dying because of my sins. The nails through his hands were there because of my sins. He was beaten and hung on that cross because of my sins. I fell to the ground in shame, weeping. Jesus called me and said, "Christy, I love you."

It felt like lightning went through every limb of my body. *He* loved me; he *loved* me; he loved *me!* The little girl whose Mommy didn't want her, whose Daddy abandoned her, whose whole family deserted her because she had sex before she was married—Jesus loved me. If Jesus loved me, then there couldn't be anything terribly wrong with me, right? God doesn't make mistakes, and Jesus loves me!

But he didn't know I'd had those two abortions. If he knew that, how could he ever love someone who did that? All of a sudden, it seemed like he took me through all the time that had gone by from that moment going forward to when I was born. I saw Roman boats then Spanish galleons, pioneers in covered wagons and trains then cars and planes and rocket ships. He looked through time from that moment, hanging on the cross, into the future where I stood. I saw myself walking out of the hospital after having the first abortion, and he was there. Then I saw myself walking out of the abortion facility in New York after having the second abortion, and he was there. He already knew that I was going to get pregnant and have two abortions. And he loved me so much, he still took my sins to the cross and died, paying the price I should have paid.

You can receive Jesus right now as your personal Savior by saying a simple prayer. God does not need fancy speeches and big words. He is waiting for you right now. Just tell him you need him. Confess your sins to him, tell him you are sorry, and ask him to forgive you. Then ask Jesus to come into your life as your personal Savior and help you to be the kind of person God wants you to be. Believe in your faith, and you will be saved.

How will you know that Jesus saved you? If you prayed sincerely and confessed your sins and asked Jesus to come into your life, there are many promises in the Bible to assure you that you are saved. In 1 John 5:11–13, it says,

> God has given us eternal life, and this life is in His son Jesus. Anyone who has the son has the life; anyone who does not have the Son of God does not have the life. These things that I have written to you who believe in the name of the Son of God, in order that you may know that you have eternal life.

John is saying if you have faith to believe what the Bible says, you will be born again and have eternal life. The moment that you received Jesus as your Savior by your faith and as an act of your will, several wonderful things happened! When you asked Jesus into your life, your sins were forgiven (Colossians 1:14), you became a child of God (John 1:12), you received the gift of eternal life in heaven (John 5:24), and you began the great adventure for which God created you (John 10:10).

Whether you believe in an afterlife or not doesn't change what the truth is. God gives us the choice of where we want to spend eternity. You are either going to live in paradise in heaven with God and his son Jesus, or you can choose not to believe in Jesus as your Savior and choose not to live in heaven. You can choose to go to hell. You can choose to live forever in hell. Hell is the name of the place where God will not be, where Jesus will not be. It will not be paradise. And God has given you this opportunity to choose. You can't buy your way into heaven, you can't pray a bunch of prayers over and over to get into heaven, and you can't do enough good works to get into heaven. There is only one way to get into heaven—believe in Jesus as your Savior.

I didn't feel any different. I didn't look any different. But I knew I was different. I was sitting there on the floor in my hotel room and knew that I had been born again, but I knew there was more. I couldn't imagine anything more wonderful than knowing God loves me. He forgave my sins, and Jesus came into my life as my personal Savior! Reverend Carothers talked about being baptized with the Holy Spirit. Any good Catholic knows that God is a trinity of God the Father, Jesus the Son of God, and God's Holy Spirit. This wasn't a new concept to grasp, but I had never been taught anything about being baptized in the Holy Spirit. I went back to the books and looked up the scriptures about this.

John wrote a great deal about the Holy Spirit. In John 14:16, Jesus told the disciples,

> If you love me, you will obey what I command. And I will ask the Father and he will give you the Holy Spirit to be with you forever—the Spirit of Truth…you know him, for he lives with you and will be in you.

And farther in the same chapter, at 14:26, Jesus said, "The Holy Spirit, whom the father will send in my name, will teach you all things and will remind you of everything I have said to you." In Acts 1:5, Jesus told us, "You will receive power when the Holy Spirit comes on you." In Acts 2, John tells us that on the day of Pentecost (the day they were baptized by the Holy Spirit), the disciples were together in a large room when the Holy Spirit came to them. "All of them were filled with the Holy Spirit and began to speak in other tongues as the Spirit enabled them" (Acts 2:5).

Then I found this scripture in Acts 11:16: "John baptized with water, but you will be baptized with the Holy Spirit." Obviously, being baptized in the Holy Spirit was different from being born again. I wasn't sure what it was all about, but I wanted everything the Lord would give me. He gave it to Reverend Carothers and others he talked about in his books, so I wanted it too.

I got back on my knees and prayed something like, "Lord God, Father, Jesus, Son of God, these scriptures tell me you'll baptize me in the Holy Spirit and that I'll speak in other tongues and that the Holy Spirit will be with me and guide me and give me power to do your will. I want to help others to come to know you and to be born again and baptized in the Holy Spirit. I ask right now that you will baptize me in the Holy Spirit."

I sat there for a few minutes. The room was cold, and it had turned dark outside. I stood up to close the curtains and turn the heat up. As I turned back around, I knew. There wasn't any banging of drums or trumpets sounding, but I knew that I was not alone in that room. I wasn't afraid. I was overwhelmed with God's love. I knew that the Holy Spirit was in that room with me. I sat down on the bed and quietly praised God for his loving-kindness, for blessing my faith, and I prayed in an unknown tongue. I was filled with the Holy Spirit—every cell, every drop of blood. Everywhere in me was filled with his love. I don't know how long I sat there in absolute wonder and joy unspeakable to be in fellowship with God.

I felt that I wasn't done yet, that there was so much more. I felt excited at the expectation in me. I found a scripture in Romans 12:1–2 that I was certain God put there just for me.

> Therefore, I urge you, brothers, in view of God's mercy, to offer your bodies as living sacrifices, holy and pleasing to God, which is your spiritual worship. Do not conform any longer to the pattern of this world but be transformed by the renewing of your mind.

I knew all about using my body for things that weren't pleasing to God. This scripture hit home for me like none other. God had been merciful to me. He had forgiven my sins and washed me clean, and I was born again. I got back on my knees and prayed in other tongues, and aloud, I asked God to accept my body as a living sacrifice. I had a little trouble with thinking I was already holy, but the Holy Spirit reminded me that's what being born again was all about, so I prayed to be holy and pleasing to God. I asked him to help me change and not conform any more to the pattern of sin that I had been lost in for so long.

As I prayed both in English and in other tongues, I knew God was touching the very darkest places in me and was changing me. I was being transformed by the renewing of my mind! The transforming was necessary to create in me a new woman of God, the person I was always supposed to be. I needed to know that there wasn't anything terribly wrong with me, and God's love proved that beyond any doubt for me.

I think it is important to explain something here. I still did not understand that the two abortions I'd had took the lives of my first two children. I was so uneducated and naive about this that I had only asked forgiveness for having sex before I was married. The Lord had plans to take me back to those horrible moments of my life and would explain to me what I had really done. At this point, as a brand-new Christian just born again moments before, newly baptized in the Holy Spirit, I was ignorant of those facts. I'll get to that in another chapter.

I was reading another scripture from 1 Corinthians 12:8, which says, "To one there is given through the Holy Spirit the message of wisdom, to another the message of special knowledge by the same Holy Spirit." I read in Reverend Carothers's books about the gifts the Holy Spirit gives us. There is wisdom, knowledge, faith; the ability to heal others, to do miracles, to prophecy, to discern spirits, to deliver a message from God in different tongues, and of interpreting messages in tongues. I wanted everything the Lord had to give me.

I prayed again and asked for a special gift from the Holy Spirit. It took some time before I was certain which of the gifts I had received. I didn't know anyone at the ski resort who was a Christian, I didn't know any churches in town that were Christian, and I was a babe in Christ. If I had someone to guide me, I might have figured it out sooner.

Looking back from now, it is obvious to me that the Holy Spirit blessed me with the gift of special knowledge. I was talking to one of the other waitresses while we set up for lunch, and she was telling me about her boyfriend and the trouble they were having. I prayed to myself and asked the Lord how I could help her. It just came to my mind. The Holy Spirit told me she was cheating on her boyfriend. The next time we talked, I suggested that she needed to be honest with him if he really meant something to her. She asked me what I meant, so I told her I knew she was cheating on him, and that had to stop.

She was shocked and said that she was certain nobody knew, and she wanted to know how I knew about it. I wasn't sure what I should tell her. I was new to this. I decided that the best thing was to just tell her that I had been born again, and I was trying to learn about this new life. I didn't know to tell her that the Holy Spirit was blessing me with the gift of special knowledge. I stumbled my way through my story and said I would pray for her. She told me later that what I had said to her really made her start thinking about what she was doing. She broke it off with the other guy, and things with her boyfriend got better.

As I read my Bible, went to Bible studies and church, and grew more in the Lord, I began to realize that this was an incredible gift. When I allowed the Lord to open the doors for me, the Holy Spirit was always faithful to bless me with the special knowledge I needed in any situation. On the other side of being abused, abandoned, adopted, almost raped at a very young age, and using sex to cover whatever it was that was wrong with me to get attention and affection, I had learned that on the other side of the life that I had been living was forgiveness, everlasting life, being born again, having Jesus as my Savior, fellowship with God, being baptized in the Holy Spirit, and that there was nothing terribly wrong with me.

CHAPTER 6

I eventually married and had a baby and continued my walk with the Lord. I became pregnant two more times but miscarried both times. This was an increasingly difficult time for me. Being able to share my grief at a ladies' Bible study or with my pastor helped me to walk through that valley and still be able to praise the Lord and trust him. He was faithful and was with me every day.

My mother had been diagnosed with breast cancer and had a mastectomy, so when I discovered a lump in my breast, I was very frightened. I went to the doctor and was sent to get an X-ray; the lump showed clearly on that X-ray. The doctor examined me, found the lump, and decided to do a biopsy and remove the lump the next day.

I went to church that evening and asked for prayer. They laid hands on me and prayed for me to be healed. I didn't sleep much that night.

When I got to the hospital the next morning, they sent me to get another X-ray then took me to the preoperation room to get prepared for the surgery. The doctor came in holding the two X-rays. He put the one that had been taken the day before and then the one they had just taken on the lightboard. He showed me where the lump was on the first X-ray and then asked me if they took the X-ray that morning of the same breast. I told him they did, and he explained that there was no lump in the X-ray they took that morning.

He did another exam and could not feel the lump. It was gone! I tried to feel it myself and could not find it. He ordered a second X-ray but of both breasts this time. There was no lump. He didn't understand, so he sent me home.

I understood. The Lord had removed the lump the night before when I had been prayed for! I hadn't felt any different. I didn't even know it had happened. As I was driving back home, I was praising the Lord and thanking him for healing me. What an incredibly awesome thing. I had experienced a miracle! As soon as I got home, I called my pastor and told him what had happened. He rejoiced with me, and we praised the Lord together.

My mother's breast cancer came back. Twenty years after her first mastectomy, she had to have a second mastectomy. She eventually would also have skin cancer and cancer in her lungs because she smoked constantly, and the cancer would get into her bone marrow and spread through her whole body. I knew that because of her breast cancers, I was at a high risk for having it too. I would eventually have seven lumps removed from my breasts; they were all benign. Except for one small spot of skin cancer on my leg (from sunburns) that was removed, I have remained cancer-free for seventy years. Thank you, Lord!

My grandmother called and told me that my grandfather was diagnosed with lung cancer and was dying. I was able to travel home and visit him. The pastor who had married me had also been there and prayed with my grandfather. My grandfather was saved and would be going to heaven, so I knew I would see him there one day, but losing the man who had taken me in when my parents abandoned my brother and me was very difficult for me. It took me a long time to grieve losing such a special man.

I have always loved animals, and I wanted to have a dog for my son to play with. A couple across the street from our rental had a pair of beautiful Doberman pinschers that they bred. When the puppies were brand-new, they invited us over to see them. I had a Doberman when I was in my mother's trailer during high school, so I was excited when they offered us a puppy. When they were old enough to leave the mother, my son picked one out. He picked a red female and named her Falina. Little did I know that that beautiful dog would one day become my closest friend and console me through a divorce.

I was having several medical issues that I had to get taken care of. I was having a lot of problems after the two miscarries, and my doctor recommended that I have a total hysterectomy. That would mean that I could not ever have any more children. I was only twenty-nine and had wanted another baby so badly. After a lot of prayer, I knew that there really wasn't any other choice, and shortly after my thirtieth birthday, I had the hysterectomy.

I had already had one knee surgery on my right knee, but it was hurting so much that I wasn't sure if I could keep working. I had injured my leg in a couple of motorcycle accidents, and I had a couple bad falls skiing that injured it again. It had always given me trouble. The first knee operation was to repair the cartilage, but now the tests showed that I had pulled the ligaments and tendons away from the bones as well. I made the arrangements for a month away so I'd have time to get everything caught up at work that I could and scheduled the surgery.

Everything went well. I was released in a cast from my hip to my ankle for a long time. I went to physical therapy to regain the strength in my leg, but I was told I would most likely end up in a wheelchair one day.

My leg was sore and was slowly healing, but I was also having trouble with my stomach, so I went back to the doctor. I was diagnosed with ulcers. That was physical pain, but there was a lot of mental stress from many trials and tribulations that I was going through. I just wanted it all to stop. I desperately needed some peace, and I needed to heal, and I needed to get a job. I was in a leg cast. How was I going to go to an interview on crutches?

The ulcers were causing me to be sick every time I ate. I had to learn how to change what I was eating. Things got very bad for me, and I struggled with overwhelming depression. This next part is for everyone who thinks that anyone who is a Christian never has any problems. Christians have all the same problems as anybody else. We don't become perfect when we become a Christian, but we are forgiven of our mistakes and sins when we take our problems to the Lord.

One day I was sitting in my car on the top of a tall cliff overlooking a river and thought how easy it would be to just take the brake off and slide over the edge and be done with everything. For a moment, being free from the physical pain that I was dealing with every day and being free from the depression and stress I was going through seemed like a solution. I sat there for a long time, crying to God to help me. I didn't see any other way out of everything that was causing me pain, both physical and mental pain. Jesus said one word to me—my son's name. I adored my son, and I really didn't want to leave him. He meant so much to me, and I wanted to be the best mom that I was able to be for him. I went back home and tried to do the best that I could, and time moved on.

On the other side of trials and tribulations, both physical and mental, the stress was taking a toll on my body. I had been able to get rid of the ulcers, but other stress-related problems developed that I would struggle with for many years. I knew that the Lord had a plan for my life, as He says in Jeremiah 29:11, "For I know the plans I have for you, plans to prosper you and not to harm you, plans to give you hope and a future." I didn't know it yet, but he was about to open the door for me to begin a ministry.

CHAPTER 7

I attended a ladies' Bible study where a woman talked about knowing someone in another city who was involved with an organization called Right to Life. I had not heard of them before and took some of the pamphlets she handed out. I knew about the Supreme Court's *Roe v. Wade* decision that had effectively legalized abortions for the full nine months of pregnancy in all fifty states. I had no idea how many abortions were being performed and searched the pamphlets for more information. I sent for the National Right to Life newspaper so I could learn more. I bought several books that explained, with graphic descriptions, how they performed abortions. I read the material with horror.

When I realized what I had allowed them to do, I was overwhelmed with guilt and remorse. My first two children were literally killed inside my womb. The first one was sliced to pieces and scrapped out of the one place that should have been the safest place to live. The second one was pulled apart into pieces and sucked out by a powerful machine while I slept.

I tried not to think about it. It was in the past, and I was a new person now, but I was having a tough time with the thoughts about what had happened. If I came across an ad in a magazine for baby diapers, I broke out in a cold sweat. My hands shook so badly that I couldn't turn the pages of the magazine. When I saw an ad on TV for baby food, I had to get up and leave the room. If I was at the grocery store and passed a lady holding a baby, I broke down. I felt like everything around me was pointing to the abortions I'd had and the babies I let them kill.

Everything seemed to be spinning out of control. I had to find out everything I could about what had happened to me. I went to a pastor someone recommended who had worked with Vietnam vets who had suffered from post-traumatic stress disorder. I told him that I'd been pregnant when I was sixteen and how my mother manipulated me into having an abortion and what the doctor did to me and how it traumatized me. I explained about the second abortion and how I had just learned what had really happened, that they killed my first two children, and I didn't understand that until just now. I was having horrible nightmares of bloody babies crying for help, how the magazine ads affected me and the ads on television. I told him about having two miscarriages and then the hysterectomy, and now I could never have any more children.

He told me he was certain that I was struggling with PTSD. He made an appointment for me to see a Christian therapist who could help. The therapist diagnosed PTSD and had a Bible study workbook for women who have had abortions. I took it home and worked through it very quickly. I came to a chapter that talked about feeling guilty. There were three scriptures to look up that changed everything for me. The first one was Psalm 38:4, "My guilt has overwhelmed me like a burden too heavy to bear." This was King David talking to God about sinning with Bathsheba. I found it incredible that a Jewish king over several thousand years ago, who had committed murder so he could take a man's wife as his own, could feel exactly like a young mother in the twentieth century who'd had an abortion. But that was exactly what I was feeling like—being overwhelmed with guilt too heavy to carry.

Psalm 32:5 says, "I acknowledged my sin to you [to God] and did not cover up my iniquity. I said, 'I will confess my transgressions to the Lord,' and you [the Lord] forgave the guilt of my sin." This was tremendous for me. Here was a scripture that had been written thousands of years ago, but it was exactly what I needed to hear. I had never asked the Lord for forgiveness for allowing them to take the lives of my two children. I knelt and prayed like I had never prayed before.

This was touching something deep inside me. There was this horrible black box in my heart where I had kept everything about those abortions. I had locked it and sealed it forever. I slowly opened the box and took those abortions out and confessed to the Lord that I had allowed them to take the lives of my first two children. God was faithful and forgave the guilt of my sins. I can't describe to you what that moment was like. I can't tell you how it felt to *know* that Jesus loved me even knowing that I had allowed them to kill my first two children. It took me a couple of days to work through all of this.

The third scripture had an even more powerful impact on me. Psalm 118:5 says, "In my anguish I cried to the Lord and He answered by setting me free." He set me free! I would suffer no more sleepless nights, cold sweats, terror, trembling in fear, guilt, or remorse for having had those two abortions. I did have regret. I regretted that I hadn't been smarter, that I should have stood up to my overbearing, lying, manipulative mother and said no. I was certain if I hadn't had the first abortion, I wouldn't have thought having another one would be so easy to solve my problems. I had a few moments of doubt that I could ever be forgiven for such horrid sins as killing my first two children. How could a holy God love me? How could Jesus love me anymore?

I found Romans 10:38–39.

> I am convinced that neither death nor life,
> neither angels nor demons, neither the present
> nor the future, nor any powers, neither height
> nor depth, nor anything else in all creation will
> be able to separate us from the love of God that is
> in Christ Jesus our Lord.

I was so humbled, thankful, and grateful that God loved me, that Jesus loved me, and to know that there is nothing that can separate me from his love.

There was another scripture that I found that touched me deeply.

> You created my innermost being; you knit
> me together in my mother's womb. I praise you

because I am fearfully and wonderfully made;
your works are wonderful; I know that full well.
My frame was not hidden from you when I was
made in that secret place. When I was woven
together in the depths of that place, your eyes
saw my unformed body. All the days ordained for
me were written in your book before one of them
came to be. (Psalm 139:13–16)

Again, I am in awe of how something that was written centuries ago can so perfectly fit what I was going through. These scriptures changed my life.

I found and attended a Right to Life meeting that was held in another town. I was so impressed by the knowledge the people there had about abortions, how abortions were supported by Planned Parenthood across the country, and how many Right to Life groups were holding nonviolent legal protests in front of facilities and hospitals that provided abortions.

I learned so much in just a couple of hours. I found out how to start our own Right to Life group in our own town and met with my mother-in-law to ask her to pray with me about doing this. We were both excited and agreed to call five other people and invite them to a meeting if they were interested. We had to have ten people to begin a Right to Life group in our town. We had many more than ten people attend our first meeting. We wanted to begin by educating ourselves with the statistics and facts so we could intelligently respond to questions about where abortions were being performed, how many in our state, and what we could do to actively participate in this important battle.

We joined another Right to Life group in another town and protested the very hospital that I had my first abortion at. The doctor that performed that abortion on me was still doing abortions there. It was one of the most fulfilling events I ever participated in. I was voted as the president of our Right to Life group, and I held meetings and spoke at the other churches, ladies' Bible studies, and anywhere I was asked to speak.

Wherever I would speak, I helped the people set up a Right to Life group and get it going. We were able to rapidly increase the number of Right to Life members in our state. Each group was unique with folks who had various levels of knowledge about abortions, and they assisted each other with bringing in speakers for educating each other, gathering literature and materials, and planning legal, non-violent protests. I was elected the vice president of the state's Right to Life organization to help oversee the incredible movement that was happening. I was invited to testify before the state senate, and I shared my story, hoping to make an impact on anyone who didn't understand how abortions can really destroy a woman. I thought it was the beginning of an important and special ministry.

My family moved to another state. I called the local Right to Life group to find out when they would be meeting. I became involved right away with speaking to various churches and assisted with getting members into the organization. Before long, I was voted in as the president of the local Right to Life group for the Denver City/County metropolitan area. I met with the pastors at the church I was attending and planned to begin a ladies' Bible study focused on healing for women who had abortions. I was invited to speak to the entire congregation at a Sunday-evening service. Several women approached me after the service and asked if they could join the Bible study. It was a successful study; the Lord healed every lady who attended from guilt, suicidal thoughts, drinking, drugs, and other abuses these women shared that they were struggling with.

Word was getting around, and I was asked to begin another group as soon as we completed the first one. I notified the church secretary to include in the upcoming bulletins that there would be another ladies' study for Post Abortion Counseling and Education. I had so many requests immediately that I knew that the Lord was working on these women's hearts. We met once a week and made excellent progress going through the workbooks and scriptures.

The Lord led me to another scripture that wasn't in the workbook, but it had quite an impact on my own healing. I was reading scriptures in the book of Joel, who was a prophet in the Old Testament. There had been a drought and a plague of locusts across the land. Joel prayed to the Lord, and God answered, saying he would send food and drink enough for everyone. He said he would drive the armies that had invaded their lands far away. The Lord said not to be afraid, but be glad and rejoice (Joel 2:18–21).

In Joel 2:25, the Lord says, "I will repay you for the years the locusts have eaten." I had never seen a locust, so I didn't think this scripture had anything to do with me. God said to me, "The locusts have eaten much of your life. You lost years to sin—your mother's sin, your father's sin, others that sinned against you, and your own sin. I will repay you for the years that locusts took from you."

Wait a minute! This scripture was saying to me that what I lost due to having two abortions, the Lord was going to repay me for that? It was too much for me to understand right then. I had to step back and think about this. How could the Lord repay me? I wasn't interested in money. What had I lost? I lost my first two children, and then I lost two more to miscarriages. I'd had a complete hysterectomy and could not have any more children, so the Lord couldn't mean that he would let me get pregnant again.

And so softly, so gently, so compassionately, Jesus spoke to me and said, "Christy, you haven't lost your children. They are here with me, waiting for when you will join us."

It was so overwhelming to think about. My four children were in heaven with God and with Jesus, and I would get to meet them and be with them and hold them and tell them how much I love them one day. That was how the Lord was going to repay me for the years that the locusts took from me!

I shared this scripture from Joel at the next ladies' Bible study, and it had the same effect on the women that it had on me. We cried together, held each other, and then we did an incredible thing. The workbook had talked about women burying their babies after having a miscarriage, so they had to name them. This gave them some closure and a way to grieve. Women who had abortions didn't have that choice. How do you ever get closure for allowing someone to take the life of your child?

We all agreed that we should name our babies. We agreed to pray about it, and at the next meeting, we went around the room and shared what we named them and why that name was special. It was an emotional session. We laughed, and we cried with each other, and at the end, we all felt we had achieved some kind of closure with our abortions. We knew that the Lord would continue to walk us through other lessons, but this was monumental for all of us.

I never knew if my babies were boys or girls, so I wanted to pick names that would work for either one. I chose Ayren for my first child because I have some Irish in me, and Aaron is an Irish male name, and Eryn is the female name. I combined them to create Ayren. I chose Bobbee and spelled it uniquely so it wouldn't identify with either male or female for my second child and Cris for the first child I miscarried. It could be Christine or Christopher, so again I spelled it without using the H to be unique. I chose Darby for the second child I'd miscarried because I had loved the movie *Darby O'Gill and the Little People*, an Irish story with one of my favorite actors, Sean Connery, as Darby O'Gill. I had also known a girl who was named Darby, so it worked for me. I named my children: Ayren, Bobbee, Cris, and Darby, and one day, I know that we will all be together for the rest of eternity.

I was speaking at every church that called the Right to Life office and requested someone to visit. I promised the Lord if He opened the doors, I would go wherever He asked me to go. I never once called anyone and asked if I could come and speak to them. I spoke somewhere almost every Sunday and many Wednesday evenings. Sometimes I'd speak at a service in the morning and drive to another church and speak at their evening service that night. I started to get calls from people who had heard me speak at their church and asked if I could start a ladies' Bible study for healing women who had abortions. I began to see that I wasn't able to be everywhere all the time. After seeking the Lord's guidance and praying with several of the key folks in the Right to Life organization, I put together a training session for folks who could set up their own Bible studies in their own churches. This worked very well. Instead of me guiding eight to ten women through the workbook at one church, there were now fifteen other leaders holding these sessions at their churches, guiding eight to ten women to healing in fifteen other churches.

A man approached me after I had spoken at his church and wanted to know if I would be interested in doing a radio talk show. He said it could be about Right to Life issues, and he would produce it. All I had to do was show up to tape it. He introduced me to another man who was a professional in the industry and had access to a facility where we could do the taping. I was certain that this was a door the Lord had opened that I was supposed to go through.

I agreed to meet them at the studio the next week to try a couple of tapings. The producer and I would go over a list of individuals in the area who were working on various projects within the Right to Life interests. My idea was to spotlight people who were out there in the community so that the folks who needed help or could donate or offer their time had someone to get in touch with.

The program was a remarkable success. By the end of the summer, my radio program was being aired on all four Christian radio stations in the Denver area seven times a week. People were getting valuable information, and the Lord was using this to reach out to people who needed help.

After taping one of my programs, the producer and the technician were very somber when I came out of the booth. Usually, after taping a show, I would leave right away and head back home. Something was telling me I needed to stay for a while. In that program that they had just heard me taping, I had talked about what an abortion can do to a woman and how men can also suffer guilt and remorse after their child has been aborted. Both men sat and told me how they had each taken a woman to have an abortion before they had become Christians. I immediately knew that the Lord was present and touching their hearts.

I listened as they shared their sorrow. Then we got down on the floor on our knees right there in the studio, and they each confessed their sins and asked the Lord for his forgiveness for those abortions. Neither of them knew where the girls were that they had been dating so many years before, but they prayed contrite and sincere hope that they would find Jesus and healing. I knew that the Lord had used what I had said in my radio program to touch those two men.

Before I left that afternoon, I knew that they had been forgiven, and a great burden had been lifted from them. It was always my prayer before I spoke or recorded a radio program that the Lord would give me the words he wanted said and that he would prepare the hearts of those listening to be blessed by those words. I was blessed knowing that others would be touched hearing that program.

The producer of my radio program was able to get an offer for me to write a weekly column about Right to Life issues in the Denver Metro Area Christian newspaper, another door I didn't go looking for that the Lord opened for me. That put me into over a million homes in the metro area. The speaking engagements increased. I was attending conventions as a keynote speaker, holding workshops about abortions and what women can suffer after having an abortion. People were getting the information, and women were being healed.

Our Right to Life group had grown and was active in holding weekly meetings outside local junior high and high schools. We weren't allowed on public school property, but we could set up tables on the sidewalks with pamphlets and invite the students who walked by after classes to listen. I joined as many of those as I could. We had girls ask about abortions and how to get one. We had girls ask what they could do for a friend who was pregnant, and occasionally, we'd have a girl shyly ask for help. I know that there were many babies saved from abortions because of this group's commitment.

The Lord opened another door that was truly a miracle. A teacher had come out to one of the tables we had at a junior high school and spoke to our group. He was a biology teacher and covered the health classes that taught sex ed. He said he could invite a speaker to come into his classes and present this information. I said I would love to do that. No Christian speaker had ever been allowed to speak to a public junior high or high school class about abortion in that school district. I agreed to meet with the principal and let them review the material I would cover. I was sternly instructed that I could not use any scriptures in my talk. It was strictly to be information about abortions and what happens when you have one. I agreed, and a date was set. I prayed with my ladies' Bible study. I met with my pastor, and we prayed together, and I prayed with the Right to Life group that I would be representing.

I felt positive about speaking to the seventh and eighth graders and was excited to have this opportunity. I would be speaking for one hour in several classes. The students were attentive and polite and asked great questions. We had good conversations in every class. Many of them had seen the tables outside but hadn't stopped. I'm sure they didn't want to be embarrassed in front of their friends. But bringing it into their classroom opened the opportunity for them to find out what it was all about. It was very successful. The Lord opened a door that had been closed to the Right to Life organization, and I am certain that there are babies who were saved from being destroyed by an abortion because I stepped through that door that day.

This opened another door that I hadn't thought about. One of the other teachers had come in to hear my presentation and was involved in getting her master's degree. She asked me about speaking to classes at the college she was attending. What an incredible opportunity to talk about abortions and to reach out to women who might be suffering after having an abortion. I spoke many times to various classes at quite a few of the colleges in the area.

On the other side of the door that the Lord opens for you will be blessings beyond anything you ever imagined. I never thought about writing a column in the newspaper or speaking to students or having a radio talk show. I was continually humbled by the Lord's blessings. I saw women blessed and grow in the Lord and be healed from horrible memories and guilt after having an abortion. I know there are many babies alive today because of the work of the many fine people I worked with at the Right to Life organizations.

CHAPTER 8

I had taken a part-time job teaching aerobics at a woman's gym near our house to bring in some additional income. I would teach a couple of classes, swim laps in the pool, and head back home each morning. After aerobics, I'd go tape my radio show or visit my next guest to prepare them and help them be more comfortable when we taped the show. I'd go to the Right to Life meetings and conduct the business of that group, then there were the weekly Right to Life educational setups we did at the junior high and high schools. I usually had one or two speaking engagements a week and the ladies' Bible studies at my church. I wrote the column for the newspaper and had to get it to the editor on time.

As I went through my week, I would receive calls from the Right to Life office with requests for speaking, events that different churches put up, and often they'd get requests for help. They received a call one afternoon from a girl who was requesting help. She said she was pregnant, and her stepfather had beaten her when he found out. She was hiding at a friend's house and gave them that address.

When I got there, I found a thirteen-year-old child. She was Hispanic. I was familiar with the Hispanic cultural. I had learned that every culture has norms and morals that can be different from others. We sat down so she could tell me her story. When she was through, she began to cry. I took her in my arms until she calmed down.

She would eventually lose the baby because her stepfather had kicked her repeatedly in the stomach purposely to make her have a miscarriage. Her mother was a drug addict and not even home when he had attacked her. I was able to give her contact information for a safe house and counseling. I suggested that she go to the police to press charges against her stepfather. I told her they would contact Family Services after taking her to the hospital to be checked out.

After she had the miscarriage, she decided to live with her biological grandparents who lived in Mexico. She called to say goodbye before she left. She was grateful for the help she received and wanted to say thank you. I wished her well and thanked her for calling. It sounded like she would have a better chance with her grandparents at growing up in a safe environment.

January 22 was the anniversary of the Supreme Court's decision on *Roe v. Wade*. I had always participated in whatever the state's Right to Life groups put together. That year, there was going to be a large rally in the park in front of the Colorado State Capitol Building in downtown Denver, with speakers standing on the famous Mile-High Steps. We hoped for five thousand to attend.

I was asked to speak that morning. There would be four speakers who would all cover abortion issues and Right to Life topics before me. I wanted to encourage the crowd. We had been fighting this battle for many years, and I wanted something special. I prayed and asked the Lord to give me the words he wanted me to share. The Lord led me to a story about William Wilberforce, a Christian Englishman who served in the parliament between 1784 to 1826. He had brought a resolution forward every year to abolish slavery that never passed while he was in parliament. Due to his failing health, he was forced to retire in 1826 but kept working on the campaign to abolish slavery. There is a statue in Westminster Abbey near his grave that praises his long labor to abolish the slave trade and slavery itself. When the Slavery Abolition Act of 1833 was finally passed, Mr. Wilberforce died three days later. He had fought the battle to abolish slavery for forty-nine years.

I started reading some of the speeches he had given over the years. I wasn't aware that many other pro-lifers had been using Mr. Wilberforce's words. I was excited about what I was reading and started to put together my speech. Here are some of the quotes I used that day. I began by explaining who he was and how long he battled to get slavery abolished. I related that to the battle we were fighting to either get *Roe v. Wade* overturned or get an amendment to the constitution. I knew many folks agreed with the Right to Life organization, but they failed to get involved. I shared this quote: "You may choose to look the other way, but you can never say again that you did not know." Then I added, "Surely the principals of Christianity lead to action as well as meditation."

I closed my speech by sharing this quote:

> Accustom yourself to look first to the dreadful consequences of failure; then fix your eye on the glorious prize which is before you; and when your strength begins to fail, and your spirits are well-nigh exhausted, let the animating view rekindle your resolution, and call forth in renewed vigor the fainting energies of your soul!

I called the crowd to make a resolution to become active in something, anything that would help bring an end to abortion. I thanked those who were already involved and active and praised them for their work. The crowd had become energized, and when I finished my speech, they clapped and cheered. A great roar went up for several minutes. The Denver newspaper reported that there had been over ten thousand people in the park for our rally. That would be the largest crowd that I had ever spoken in front of before. It was exhilarating to read how successful it had been.

The churches in the area put together a convention each year. They designed it to be a weeklong event, and each year, it focused on different topics. They brought in keynote speakers and topic experts who put on workshops each day. They wrapped it up by having services covering the topics in each of their own churches at the end of the week. I received a call from the coordinator and was invited to teach workshops, to be part of an open Q and A panel, and to be the opening-night keynote speaker. The topic was "Issues for Christian Families." They would focus on abortion the first day, divorce one day, drugs/addiction one day, music and pop culture influences one day, and the gay and lesbian influences on the final day. I was already hearing the opening speech in my head.

The week before the convention was scheduled to begin, I received a phone call at my home. It was from a man I did not recognize, and he did not give me his name. He told me that I had to cancel my engagements at the convention immediately. I asked him why I would do that; it had been advertised for several weeks on the radio, television, in the newspapers, and in all the churches, so I assumed he knew about my involvement from the advertising. His response shocked me. He said that the gay community was rallying to protest the convention every day and that I didn't want to be caught in the violence. There was an author who wrote a book about how the gay movement in America was a direct attack on the American family. He had been invited to speak on the final day. The gay community wanted to not only disrupt his event, but they wanted to destroy the whole week. I asked him what he meant by the violence he spoke about. He just said that I didn't want to be caught there and said that I would be sorry if I didn't pull out of the meetings.

After he hung up, I was just shaking. I met with the convention leadership the next day and told them what had happened. I wasn't the only one who got a call. Several others who were in the advertisements had been called and threatened like I had been. They decided to contact the police, who came right over to speak to us. They took this very seriously and asked if they could put a tap on our home phones. We all agreed to have our phones tapped. I agreed not to pull out of the convention.

There was a protest going on when we arrived. Many men had tried to join hands and make a human chain to keep people from entering the parking areas, but the police were there in force and ensured that we got through and parked safely. I spoke to one of the officers about how we could keep them from entering the center and disrupting the meetings and workshops. They assured me that they had taken care of it. We had no incidents, except the picketing outside. I met many people that day who were interested in what was happening, and we made many connections. The Q and A session was excellent, and each of my workshops were standing room only. The rest of the week went just as smoothly without any further incidents.

Later that year, we moved back home and got divorced. I started putting out résumés for full-time work. I had gotten several interviews but no offers. I was becoming depressed and unsure of what was going to happen next. I had been attending a wonderful Christian church that I had spoken at several years before and was attending an adult Bible study during the week. I had been shaken by having to leave the ministries that God had opened for me. I wanted to be in his will, but I was not sure what that was anymore.

I had to move out of the rental and store all my furniture. My grandmother let me move in with her in her tiny apartment. I slept on her couch and put a bar across the back seat of my car to hang my clothes.

The week before Memorial Day, my stepsister called from Coeur d'Alene, Idaho, and asked me to come over for the weekend. Her boyfriend had a boat, and they were going to water ski all weekend. I was depressed because I wasn't getting much back on the résumés I had sent out, and there didn't seem to be many new jobs opening each week. I could stay at my father's house, so the only thing it would cost me was the gas to drive over and back. I decided it sounded too good to pass up and took off for Idaho.

My father had been divorced and remarried three times. He'd had four children with his second wife, and they were all in Coeur d'Alene. It was good to get to see them again. My father and I had been working on having a relationship over the years. I had learned to forgive him, but I still struggled with the scriptures that said we were supposed to honor our fathers and mothers. He was a big man, stood over six feet tall, and the best way that I can explain him is to say he was jolly. He laughed all the time, enjoyed having his family around him, loved having me there, and was happy that I had agreed to visit. That was nice.

The next morning, my stepsister had to open the shop she worked at and be there until noon, so we made plans that I would meet her at noon, and we'd go waterskiing. I showed up wearing the top to my two-piece swimsuit with a big shirt over it, some cutoff jeans, and my tennis shoes. I braided my hair to keep it out of my face. I had no makeup on, no jewelry, no earrings, and nothing fancy because I was going to spend the day in the water.

When I got to my sister's shop, she was all excited about me interviewing with one of the owners of another shop in the resort mall. I said I could do that…tomorrow. She said he was there right now, waiting for me. I said, "Look at me! I'm in my swimsuit and cutoffs. This isn't how I go to interviews." So I went and did the interview with him. He was a delightful man and obviously understood why I was dressed that way. My stepsister had given him a heads-up. The job was for a manager of the shop he owned, and he wanted me to start right away. I hadn't brought any work clothes with me, so he agreed that I could start the following week after I drove back to Montana to get my things. It was stunning. I had been trying for several months to get a job back home, and nothing opened for me there. Here I was, one day in Coeur d'Alene, and I had a fantastic job with good pay waiting for me. When the Lord closes a door, he always opens the one he wants us to walk through.

I talked it over with my father. He and his wife offered to let me stay with them until I could find a place of my own. I told him I had a dog that I would be bringing, and he offered to build a dog run for me outside because he didn't like the idea of having a Doberman in his house. They had six bedrooms and three bathrooms with only the two of them living there at the time. I accepted their offer, took the job, and drove back to Montana to get my things.

I found a perfect mobile home with a large fenced yard for Falina, a master bedroom with a bath, and at the other end of the trailer was another large bedroom and bath that my son would have. He had agreed to live with me and would start college there in Coeur d'Alene. I loved my job. I got to be creative and fix up window displays and different displays in the shop. It was a high-end sportswear shop at the resort on the lake. I didn't see many local people shopping there, but I did get to meet many of the celebrities who stayed at the resort.

I would get to Falina each evening after work, and we'd run for three or four miles; sometimes we would go five miles. She patiently waited all day for me to get home, and when she saw my car pull into the driveway, she started dancing. I enjoyed her so much. She and I cuddled up on the couch and watched TV until bedtime. She slept on the bed with me too.

I met and went out with a few guys over the summer. I really wasn't in a hurry to do any dating because I was enjoying being single. I had found a wonderful church and had been attending there, and I was getting close to the pastor and his wife. Occasionally, when I didn't have to close the shop on Wednesdays, I attended their adult Bible study too. My father had attempted several times to get me to come back to the Catholic church, and I did go a couple of times with him, but I made it clear that I would not be joining the Catholic church again.

The real estate agent who helped me find a place to rent that would take a dog told me about a man who was the son of a couple she knew from her church. He owned his own business in town, and she thought he was our age. She gave me the address, and I realized I had been driving right past it every day on my way to work and again on my way home at night. I didn't go by for a while, but one day on my way home, I decided to stop. I hoped he would be a Christian and tall; I am five feet seven inches tall. I was taller than all the boys from sixth grade until I got into high school, so I guess I was a little sensitive about being too tall.

I had no idea what this guy looked like. The store he owned was a sports shop that sold hunting gear, fishing equipment, camping things, licenses, and army-navy surplus items. It looked interesting as I pulled up and parked. When I walked in, there were a couple of people at one end of the store, but I didn't see anybody behind the counter. I took a couple of steps toward the fishing gear when someone behind me said, "May I help you?"

I turned around and lost my breath. I couldn't speak! A tall, muscular man, who obviously lifted weights because his chest and arms were solid muscle, stood there with the most delightful grin. He was tanned. I bet he ran outside like I did, and he was wearing a pair of shorts and a tight T-shirt, socks, and tennis shoes. I noticed his legs were also muscled and tanned, but it was his deep-blue eyes that melted me. I could not speak. That doesn't happen to me very often.

I stammered something about needing some fishing hooks because my son was visiting that weekend, and we were going fishing together. I walked over to the wall display of fishing hooks and line, sinkers, and bobbers and tried to catch my breath. I remember telling myself to get a grip! But he was so good-looking, and I didn't care if he was the guy my friend knew or not. I wanted to get to know this guy better.

I picked out several packages of hooks as he stepped behind the counter and sat on a small stool behind the cash register and waited. The other customers had left, so it was just us in the store. He said something about it being time to close, so I hurried and put my items on the counter. He flashed me the most beautiful smile, and I am almost certain his big blue eyes were watching everything I did. He was flirting with me. I wasn't sure if I even remembered how to flirt back.

Suddenly, it dawned on me that I might not be looking my best. I had just come from work and wondered if I looked all right. I was wearing a tight pair of white capri pants with a bright-yellow shirt and white sandals. I was tanned and slim from spending my evenings running in the summer sun with Falina, swimming in the lake, waterskiing with my stepsister and her boyfriend, and riding Jet Skis on the weekends. My naturally light-brown hair was sun bleached and reached almost to my waist. I decided that was as good as I was going to get for a thirty-nine-year-old.

I paid for my things. Noticing he didn't wear a wedding ring, I boldly asked him if he'd like to have dinner with me. At first, he looked a little stunned, but then he smiled that gorgeous smile and said he'd love to have dinner with me. He asked me where we were going to eat, and I said I was new to town and asked if he knew of a nice place. He walked over to the window and pointed to a Mexican restaurant down the street. He said he had to close the store first, but I could go on down there and get us a table, and he'd be right down. I asked him what his name was and told him mine. He locked the door behind me, and I drove down the street to the restaurant.

I told the guy at the restaurant that I was meeting someone when he asked where I wanted to sit. I could see a patio outside the back of the restaurant with brightly colored umbrellas over tables. It was a beautiful evening, so I chose to sit outside. When I was seated, there were a lot of bees flying around. The waiter said someone had spilled their margarita earlier, which had attracted the bees. He offered to grab a hose and spray it off. I said sure and started helping shoo the bees away. I didn't notice that the Big Man had arrived and stood looking for me from the front door. When he spotted me wildly swinging a napkin around and the waiter spraying water all over the place, he thought, *Oh no, I've met a crazy woman.* But he wandered out to see what was going on. I explained about the spilled drink and the bees and that I was trying to swat them away so we could eat outside.

After a delightful dinner, which I fully remembered how to flirt through, he offered to drive me out to another lake that was just north of Lake Coeur d'Alene. We parked on a dike close to the water and watched a beautiful full moon rise and sparkle in the water in front of us. We enjoyed getting to know one another, asking all the questions people asked, like, "Where are you from? How did you get here? Where do you work?"

Then he asked one that I didn't realize had caused him some concern. He had heard me say back in his store that my son was coming for the weekend. I wasn't wearing a wedding ring, but that must have bothered him a little bit. He asked how old my son was. I told him my son was nineteen and coming to live with me and go to college here. I explained that I was divorced. He immediately gave me that great big smile and flashed those exquisite blue eyes at me. I melted all over again.

I was about to ask if he wanted to go to a movie or something the next weekend, but a bright light shined in the window. We had stopped in a popular parking place that the teenagers used, and the local policeman had stopped to see what was going on. The look on his face was priceless when he shined his light on two thirty-something-year-old adults talking. We laughed all the way back to where my car was parked at the restaurant. It had certainly been a fun and surprising evening.

I gave him my phone number and said I'd love to do it again sometime. He quickly asked if I liked car shows. I told him I remembered my father building hot rods when I was a kid, and yes, I loved going to car shows. He said there was a large one the next weekend over in Spokane, about forty minutes away, and he asked if I'd like to go with him. I said that I would love to go with him.

My son had something come up and wasn't able to make it over that weekend, so I felt better about making plans to go to the car show with the Big Man. We had so much fun. There were hundreds of beautiful classic cars to see. I told the Big Man that my first car had been a 1969 Camaro convertible pace car painted white with orange stripes across the trunk and hood and a black-and-orange houndstooth interior. I explained that it had been sold and that I was still grieving over my loss. I loved that car.

He seemed very impressed. Then he told me about the car he owned, a 1957 Chevrolet Bel Air two-door hardtop. He said it was his first car, which he bought when he was sixteen, and that he still owned it. All I ever saw him drive was a pickup truck, so I had no idea he owned such an iconic car. He told me it was in storage, and he'd be happy to show it to me if I wanted to see it. He said it was badly in need of being restored and repainted. I said I would love to meet his beauty.

A few days later, we met at the storage facility, and he unlocked the door and pushed it up. He got in and started the car up and pulled it out into the sunshine. And there right in front of me was an incredible 1957 Chevy Bel Air! He was right. It needed to be repainted. He explained that the last paint job he'd done had been lacquer paint, and lacquer paint cracks over time. Even with the cracks, I could see it had been taken care of, and I fell in love right there with that beautiful car. She would become one of our favorite joys together.

The mobile home I had rented was only a few blocks from the Big Man's store, so he would come over after closing the store and have dinner with me most evenings. At first, I wasn't sure how he would react to my having a Doberman pinscher. I didn't know that he loved dogs too, and he would get right down on the floor and play with Falina until they both were out of breath. The Big Man would roll around and wrestle with her while I fixed dinner. I'd look in the front room, and all I'd see was her long legs and him all tangled up with her, and they were both laughing. She absolutely fell in love with the Big Man. When she'd be outside in the yard and see his truck pull up and park, she'd start to wiggle and dance until he got inside, and the wrestling would start.

I still had some furniture and things stored in Montana and needed to take a run over to finish getting everything to Coeur d'Alene. The Big Man offered to come over each night and take Falina for her walks while I was gone and make sure she got food and water. They had a fun time together, and I was relieved that she loved him like she did. I was beginning to have serious feelings for the Big Man too. He had been married before, like I had, but he didn't have any children.

One of the hardest things I ever did was to tell him that I couldn't have any more children because he would sometimes mention how he'd like a son or daughter. If he was having serious feelings about me, I needed him to know that I couldn't have children. We talked long into the night after I told him. I felt like I had given him shocking news, and I thought he might never come back. Instead, he said that my son was an incredible young man, and he would love to get to know him better. I wasn't sure exactly what that meant, but at least he wasn't running out of my life.

A few nights later, we had gone out with some friends for dinner, and when he dropped me off at my place, we kissed each other good night, and he took off for his place. After I went inside, I couldn't find Falina. It was cold out, and she usually came right away. I walked out into the backyard and found her lying on the sidewalk. I picked her up and carried her into the house. She was spitting foam from her mouth, her eyes rolled back, and she was barely breathing. I immediately called an all-night emergency vet for help. He didn't seem to think there was anything too terribly wrong and refused to come and look at her. I offered to bring her to his facility, but he told me to wait a few hours and call him back if she didn't get any better.

I tried to get her to drink a little water. I sat on the floor and held her in my lap, and she looked up at me, licked my face, and died. My heart broke. She had been with me since we got her when she was six weeks old.

I called the Big Man. When I told him what happened, he came back to my place. He sat on the floor with me and held me all night long while I cried and dozed in his arms. In the morning, he asked what I wanted to do with her. We decided to take her up to a place in the mountains where I had taken her for runs. We could bury her there. I got an old blanket, and he wrapped it around her long legs and carried her out to his truck.

As I watched him digging her grave in the frozen ground, I sat on a log and cried. It had started to snow, and I was shivering. I watched him carefully wrap her up and gently place her at the bottom of the hole. He tucked the blanket all around her, then he softly patted her head and said, "I'm sorry to have to leave you here, girl."

I watched him fill the grave and then place some large rocks all around it so other animals couldn't dig it up. I realized, watching him take such care and be so gentle with her, that I had fallen in love with this Big Man.

The next weekend, he took me hiking around the end of the lake in one of the mountain parks. It got a little chilly, but it was worth it because we saw some bald eagles up there. We stopped at a quaint little old place that was called the Fish Bar. It was called that because it was built and painted like a huge fish. There was a fire going in a big old stone fireplace, and it was cozy. While we waited for our food, the Big Man leaned over and asked me if I'd like to be sitting next to him in our porch swing growing old together. Wait, what? I think he just proposed to me! I looked into those beautiful blue eyes and simply said yes.

We started making plans for a summer wedding. Since we had both had the traditional wedding before, neither of us wanted anything like that again. We found a special little house across the street from a big park full of beautiful tall pine trees. We bought the house, and I moved in the week before our wedding. We decided to be married in the park, which wasn't traditional. I bought a gorgeous emerald-green lace dress to wear instead of a white dress.

We invited all our families and knew we would have fifteen nieces and nephews. I told them all that this was going to be a casual event in the park. I didn't want to hear one parent say to one child, "Sit down and be quiet!" I had heard that every Sunday in every church I ever went to. I wanted children to see that a Christian event could be fun.

We filled a huge box full of toys for them to play with. There was a basketball court, so we bought a basketball. There were horseshoe pits, so we got some horseshoes. We bought a bunch of bubbles with big bubble blowers. We got Frisbees and nerf footballs.

The ceremony would be held in the large gazebo. If it rained, it was big enough to keep us from getting wet. Instead of getting a wedding cake—with fifteen kids running around—I got several dozen cupcakes. My family in town offered to put together a potluck meal so I wouldn't have to try to pay for a huge dinner. I made a large potato salad and got plates and napkins and plasticware. We got several big coolers and filled them with lemonade, ice tea, soda pop, and ice.

When we picked up the marriage license and spoke to the pastor who would marry us, I found out that the maid of honor was my witness, but I didn't have to choose a female. It could be anyone who knew me. I asked my son if he would be my witness and stand up for me. He said he'd do it; that certainly wasn't traditional. The Big Man asked his father to stand up for him. We wouldn't have any bridesmaids or groomsmen because we were getting married in a park, not a church. Everyone would just be seated under the gazebo and wait for us to walk across the street.

On our wedding day, the weather was perfect, sunny but not too hot. My big brother came from Montana with his three kids. My mother came too. My father had time to attend this ceremony; he had missed my first wedding. All four of his kids to his second wife came with their various boyfriends, girlfriends, spouses, and children. My boss brought his wife and kids, and several of the men I worked with also came. The Big Man's parents were so proud. His sister came and brought his niece. It was a perfect day, and we had a perfect wedding and a wonderful time. His parents had given us airplane tickets for a trip to San Francisco for a wedding gift, but we couldn't go until a week after the wedding. We spent a wonderful week moving the Big Man into the cute little house with me.

We had so much fun in San Francisco. We went to a Giant's game, ate on Fisherman's Wharf, toured Alcatraz Island, and even drove over the Golden Gate Bridge and walked through the redwoods. Then we drove down the coast to Monterey. We ate at Clint Eastwood's café, walked along Cannery Row from the John Steinbeck novel, drove around the famous 17-Mile Drive to Pebble Beach, and spent a day at the Monterey Aquarium. The time passed too fast, and we were soon on our way back home.

I had learned several things about my new husband, the Big Man, and we had so many things in common. We loved classic cars, we loved motorcycles, we loved car racing, we loved the ocean, we loved aquariums, we loved road trips, we loved baseball, we loved football (he was a die-hard Raiders fan—my favorite players were Joe Montana, Johnny Unitas, and Dan Marino, and I would add Brett Favre, Peyton Manning, and Drew Brees over time), we loved hiking, we loved swimming, we loved good music, and we loved having conversations over good food in pleasant environments. I was falling in love more each day with my new husband.

We tried several different churches, and since my father-in-law sang in their church's choir, we often attended their church too. They had a Christmas Eve service that my father-in-law sang in, so we always went out to dinner and then met them at their church. I had been invited to speak at the Mother's Day service at the little church I first attended. They wanted me to make a presentation during the morning service. I hadn't spoken since the convention in Denver when I was threatened. When I got divorced, I changed my name for that reason. I thought I was safe, so I accepted the invitation. It was one of the only times my father didn't go to the Catholic church. He came to hear me speak. I was very touched by that even if I knew he'd go to the Catholic church that evening.

I was excited to have the opportunity and felt the speech went well, until after the service when a woman approached me and said she had heard me speak in Denver when she visited her sister. She knew my name was different. I explained I had been divorced and remarried.

Eventually, the Big Man and I found a church that we liked. There was another couple we knew from car shows who also attended. It was good to have friends going to the same church.

On the other side of divorce, taking a hit to my self-esteem because I couldn't find a job, fighting depression and stress-related problems, the Lord was faithful and blessed me with a new home, a new job, and eventually a loving Christian husband. Life was so sweet and blessed. To everyone who might be struggling after going through a divorce, I promise you that if you trust Jesus and that it is his plan for you to find someone else, there is someone else that the Lord has for you, and you will be blessed. There is a better life after divorce, a blessed life with the Lord.

CHAPTER 9

I knew that I would never be able to make any more than I already was without a college degree, so I started taking classes. My new husband was exceptionally supportive. I'd come home, and he'd have a warm dinner in the oven and had washed a load of clothes for me and folded them so neatly and left them on my dresser. I'd be doing homework until 2:00 a.m., and he'd come get me and make me go to bed. When I became overwhelmed with house-cleaning chores, homework, stress at my job and just start crying, he would be there with kind words, sweet kisses, and encouragement. I made it through the first four years with a double major in business management and human resources administration. Then he helped me decide that I could keep going and get my master's degree. It took three more years, and I graduated with a 4.0 GPA (straight As) and a master's degree in human resources development. I couldn't have achieved these incredible accomplishments without his constant support and help. A week after I graduated, I applied for and accepted an offer as assistant vice president and human resources manager at a bank. I more than doubled what I had been making while I was getting my degrees.

We decided to have the 1957 Chevy restored. One of my husband's oldest friends owned a car repair shop in Los Angeles. My husband had worked there over the years, doing paint and bodywork. He was the only person my husband trusted to work on his car. They had worked on hot rods together ever since they had been in high school. In fact, they had painted the Chevy two times already.

We made the arrangements to have the Chevy hauled to his shop, and my husband flew down to go over what he wanted done.

He brought back a picture of the Chevy after they had gotten it and started on it. There were thousands of parts and pieces lying across the floor of the shop, and I was certain they'd never get them all back together again. It took five years because we couldn't afford to pay for everything all at once. My husband would tell his buddy to go ahead and get the bumpers rechromed and the stainless steel polished. We'd pay for that, and then we'd have to decide to do work on the engine or the transmission next. It went like that until all the mechanics got completed. We powder-coated the frame black because my husband had chosen to paint the car all black this time, and they quickly reassembled the body on the frame and installed the engine and new transmission. The Big Man had to decide what kind of wheels he wanted, what size wheels, what kind of tires, and what he wanted for the interior. He took another trip to LA to look at fabric and talk to the upholsterer to get things finished up.

The day finally came when his buddy called and said the car was finished and on its way back to us. When the truck pulled up next to our house, we were both excited. I stood back and let my husband work with the truck driver to get the car backed out of the trailer. Once it was on the street, we paid the hauler and moved the car into our garage. My husband spent a long time looking over every inch, every bolt, and every emblem. The black paint was exquisite. It was more like looking into a black mirror than at the side of a car. It didn't look anything like it had in the yellow lacquer. The black showed off the beautiful lines of the body, and I was in awe of the work that had created this incredible beauty. We called my in-laws to come over and see the car; my father-in-law had taken my husband to buy it when he was sixteen, so it was just as special to him as it was to my husband. My father and his wife came over to see it too. My father had worked on hot rods when he was younger, so he appreciated a good-looking car.

We made plans to enter the car in some local car shows. Each evening during the week after we got home from work, we'd spend time out in the garage, getting her ready for the show. My job was to vacuum the interior, wash and polish the chrome wheels, clean the tires, clean the stainless steel pieces on the sides, and polish the chrome bumpers. The Big Man hand polished and buffed the paint and made sure everything in the engine was clean and polished to perfection.

The first show we went to was an indoor show at the Spokane fairgrounds. This was a large show, with over two hundred vehicles and motorcycles. We took home a Best-in-Class trophy. Unfortunately, on the way home, it rained. My Big Man was incredibly upset. I made a stupid comment that it was only water. I spent the next weekend on my back on the cement floor of our garage under the car, using Q-tips to clean all the water spots off the beautiful chrome and painted parts that had gotten wet. You can be sure I never made that mistake again.

We spent the next three years going to car shows across Idaho and Washington. One of my favorite shows was the Ford Classic Car Show that was held north of Spokane. It was a charity show. You bring some canned goods as the entry fee. We had started to attend only shows that gave something back to the community and supported some charity. We had called them to make sure they would allow a Chevy to enter their show. They said, "Sure! Come on over and join the fun."

We took home the Best-in-Class trophy…for our Chevy…at the Ford Car Show! We had joined a car club and had a ball setting up that car show. We called my husband's buddy in LA who did the restoration work and asked him to come up and go to a show with us. We laughed and looked at beautiful cars all day. It was another trophy that day for the beautiful Chevy. Over the next three years, we brought home more trophies for best of show, best paint, best Chevy, and best Tri-Five ('55, '56, '57). We made so many friends and enjoyed hearing all the stories about their beautiful cars.

My father-in-law had struggled with a heart condition and had a pacemaker implanted. Then he was diagnosed with lung cancer. He got through the surgery and recovered, but he was in and out of the hospital for the next few years. For a while, he was able to join us at some of the car shows we took the Chevy to. He enjoyed visiting with people and loved seeing all the beautiful cars. My husband and I had bought a season pass to watch the Spokane baseball team play.

One afternoon when my husband had to work, I took my father-in-law to a game. We hooted and hollered and laughed and ate hot dogs, and he even snuck in a beer. I enjoyed watching him have so much fun, and it is one of my favorite memories of him. My husband wanted to take his father for a ride in the Chevy. We picked him up and put him in the front seat and drove around. I have beautiful pictures of him enjoying that last ride in the Chevy.

When my mother-in-law became unable to care properly for him, my husband and I moved into their house. We could see him growing weaker and having more difficulties each day. When my husband and I were both at work, my father-in-law started choking and struggling to breathe. My mother-in-law called the ambulance. We met the ambulance as it arrived at the hospital, and we were able to walk to the emergency room with him. I took his hand and leaned down close to his ear and told him I was praying for him. He had a tube in his throat and couldn't talk. He squeezed my hand. He was admitted to the hospital. After they got him settled into his room, I wanted to let my husband have some time alone with his father. I leaned over and kissed him on his cheek and said good night. He patted my hands tenderly. It was the last time I saw him alive.

Because my father-in-law was a veteran of WWII, they played taps at his funeral with a recorded twenty-one-gun salute. We drove the Chevy to the funeral and parked it right in front of the church to honor him. I had several conversations with my father-in-law about being saved and knowing Jesus and going to heaven. He had asked Jesus to come into his life and be his personal Savior many years before. I tried to comfort my husband by letting him know that he would get to see his father again one day in heaven.

My mother had retired and moved back to Great Falls. She and my grandmother seemed to be getting along better than I'd ever seen them before. They both had a sense of humor and together could be hilarious to be with. I talked with my grandmother to be sure she was fine with everything my mother was doing. We both knew she could be difficult, that she would lie to your face and steal whatever wasn't nailed down. My grandmother told me that my mother had borrowed $10,000 and tried to open her own business. My grandmother had several certificates of deposit that she used to help pay for her medical expenses, and my mother took one of them. The business didn't do so well, so my grandmother lost everything. My mother never paid her back any of that money.

My grandmother had her ninetieth birthday coming up, and I wanted to give her a nice party. I called my little cousin who lived in town, and we put together a big event. It was held indoors poolside at one of the larger hotels in town, and we invited everyone we could think of. We took a lot of pictures of all the families, and my grandmother had a great time. My aunt was there with both of my cousins who had skied with us, families from each of my grandmother's brothers and sister were there and many of the neighbors who knew her. Of course, my big brother was there with my sister-in-law and their three children. The Big Man and I had to bring our doggie and our cockatiel. My grandmother had a conure, a small parrot, and we introduced her bird to our bird and laughed at their silly antics. It was an enjoyable time for everyone. From then on, the family got together each year for my grandmother's birthdays.

My mother had some recurring medical issues and was in and out of the hospital as she got older. My brother called and said she'd been taken to the hospital and was in some kind of coma. He had worked as a ski instructor and ski patrol and eventually became the director of the ski school on the same mountain we had learned how to ski on. He managed the ski races there each year and was in the middle of one of the races, so he couldn't get to town to be with our mother. The Big Man and I left Coeur d'Alene and headed for the hospital.

We arrived late that evening and found my mother. Her head was bandaged. She was hooked up to several machines that were all making strange sounds. She was still in a coma. A doctor came to speak to us. He was blunt and said that my mother's brain had swollen so badly that they really didn't expect her to live to the morning. If she did live, they expected her to have severe brain damage and would require her to be bedridden for the rest of her life.

The doctor told us he'd call us if there was any change, so we spent the night at my mother's apartment. The next morning, when we returned to the hospital, my mother was still alive but still in a coma. We knew she might be in a coma for a long time. The Big Man had to get back to work, and I had my mother's car to use, so I stayed to be with my mother. I had taken a week off work and decided I could be with her that long. After that, if there was no change, we'd have to move her to a care facility. I had learned that I could obey God's commandment to "honor your father and your mother" (Exodus 20:12). I was there, seeing to her care, and that was honoring her. I knew that she had professed to be an atheist for many years. She would not allow us to talk about the Lord or Jesus or being saved. She just flat didn't want to hear it. As I prayed for her, I was certain that the Lord was telling me I was to witness to her again. My brother and his wife and I had attempted to speak to her about salvation, and she had always laughed at us and told us we could believe whatever we wanted, but we needed to leave her alone.

The next morning when I arrived at the hospital, they had moved my mother to another room. They said she was coming out of the coma and that I could speak to her. They told me she was not fully responsive but was showing signs that the swelling in her brain was going down. If she regained consciousness, we would know what degree of brain damage she had suffered. I sat by her bed, held her hand, and softly prayed.

Sometime that afternoon she opened her eyes and said hello. I called the nurse, who called the doctor. After a quick exam, the doctor said she was recovering, and he was surprised. He had expected a brain-damaged woman who couldn't speak or walk, but my mother was able to communicate and articulate just fine. Within another day, she was able to eat, get up, and go to the bathroom, and she wanted a shower and to wash her hair. The nurses said I could help her take a shower but that I was not to leave her alone. I got her into the water and washed her hair. I got her clean and rinsed, dried off and back into a clean gown. Someone had changed the sheets on her bed while we were in the shower and had brought a lunch tray. She was coming back slowly and started cussing and complaining.

As she was flipping through channels on the TV, looking for something to watch, she came to a Christian channel and stopped.

I was stunned because she would never tolerate anything about God before. She listened for a few minutes then asked me if I understood what the preacher was talking about. He was talking about being saved so I said I understood it. She asked me what it meant. I gave her the whole message about God's love for us, sending his Son, Jesus, to pay for our sins so we could know that we would live for eternity with him in heaven.

She didn't stop me like she had always done before, and she asked some intelligent questions. She asked me why I believed it, and I told her how I read the two books. I told her at that time I was certain that there had to be more to life than having sex, getting pregnant, having an abortion, having sex, getting pregnant, and having an abortion. I talked about how I had always believed that God was real. I didn't know what to say because she had always said God was made up.

Then she said the most incredible thing to me. She said she always knew God was real, but she was angry with him for all the horrible things she had to go through in her life. I carefully talked about God giving us free will and that some of her choices hadn't been the best thing to do, so some of the things that had happened to her were her own fault. I had never spoken to my mother like this, and I quickly prayed that the Holy Spirit would continue to give me the right words.

She was getting tired and was falling asleep. She was sedated with something, so I went back to her apartment and prayed. The next day, she was back to her old self. When I got to the hospital, all the nurses were upset at her cussing and screaming at them. I could hear her as soon as I got off the elevator. One of the nurses begged me to do something to shut her up.

When I walked into her room, she acted like she hadn't seen me the day before and wanted to know why I was there. I sat down on the bed and told her how I'd been there all week, that my husband had come over too, but he had to get back to work. I told her that the doctors had said she might never come out of the coma. I told her how her brain had swollen so badly that they thought she would be brain damaged if she ever did wake up. I laid it all out for her, and she didn't seem to like anything I said.

When a nurse came in with a fresh container of water and ice, my mother started to yell at her. I looked right at my mother and told her to stop acting that way. The nurses were there to help her, and she had no right to be yelling at them. She just looked at me like she wanted to poke daggers in my eyes, but she shut up. I asked her if she wanted to take a shower and said I could help her if she wanted. She got up, and I helped her into the bathroom. She got into the shower, and I let the nurses know, so they put clean sheets on her bed. When she was dressed in a clean gown and back in the clean bed, she seemed to calm down some.

They brought her lunch tray in, and she was able to feed herself. I said I'd go down to the cafeteria and grab something. When I stepped out of her room, a couple of nurses came up to me and thanked me for getting my mother into her shower and back to bed. They said they had several extra trays, and I could have one if I wanted, so I took a tray back to my mother's room, and we had a nice lunch together. She was in a better mood. I asked her if she remembered our conversation from yesterday about being saved. I thought she might blow up again, but she became subdued and just shook her head that she remembered. I asked if she wanted to hear any more about Jesus and salvation. She shook her head that she did, so we talked about how to be saved. I got right to the point of asking her if she wanted to pray for salvation. She said that she did but not right then. I wondered if she wanted to privately pray after I left, so I just said she could let me know if she wanted me to pray with her. She said she would.

The next day when I got to her room, my grandmother was there, and so was my big brother and his wife. My mother wanted to go home, but the doctor had told my brother that he was not comfortable releasing our mother unless she had someone to stay with her because her brain was still swollen, and she could go back into a coma. He was certain she couldn't live by herself or take care of herself any longer.

My sister-in-law had suspected this could happen and had researched several assisted-living homes that my mother's Medicare income would afford. We spent the afternoon visiting them so we could go back and let our mother know what was out there. It didn't go over very well with our mother. She didn't want to move out of her apartment and said she didn't need assistance and she flat told all of us to go to hell. Then she made a comment that was exactly what I expected my mother to make. She told her mother, her son, her daughter-in-law, her daughter, and her niece that the things she had spent her life collecting —her furniture, artwork, and things in her apartment—meant more to her than any of us, and we could all go to hell. I had just spent the week taking her to the toilet, giving her showers, washing her hair, and I wasn't making any income while I was there. I'd had enough and got up and walked out. It was the last time I saw my mother alive.

I had told my brother and sister-in-law about my conversations with my mother about being saved and how she had stopped me when I asked her to pray. I knew that they would pray for her and continue to minister to her. Like me, my big brother felt the importance of honoring our mother, but neither of us enjoyed being around her. We just didn't like her. She had always been selfish, self-centered, mean, crude, potty-mouthed, and she lied constantly.

My brother would stop by her apartment when they were in town and bring her elk steaks, roasts, and hamburger. They always had tags at the ranch and would have fresh elk meat. He'd tell me when he visited her over the next two years that she got meaner and nastier. I did not call her; I felt that if the things in her apartment were so precious to her, she could have them. She didn't need me. It was an ambivalent time for me. She had hurt me so many times throughout my life that I just couldn't do it anymore.

My brother felt the same way, but for him, I think he felt giving her meat and dropping off food was honoring her the best way he could. Every time they brought up the Lord or Jesus, she told them she didn't want to hear it.

She lived for two more years, then she died alone in her apartment. I went over to help take care of removing her things and getting the apartment cleaned. My brother and I had terrible feelings, and we didn't even know how to express what we were going through. My sister-in-law was so patient with us and prayed with me and prayed with her husband, and we all prayed with each other. The best way I can explain it would be to say that we both felt we had been so hurt by this woman all our lives, and now she was dead, and we just didn't feel we'd had the opportunity to settle things between us. My brother might say it a different way.

We held a service with a born-again pastor who gave a beautiful sermon about being saved. My mother would have gotten up and walked out. But that service wasn't for her; it was for anyone in the audience who didn't know the Lord, so my mother's life in the end had a beautiful purpose, and we prayed for our families who were there. Standing at the grave site of my grandfather and my uncle, my grandmother placed her daughter next to her son and commented that a mother shouldn't have to bury her children. I put my arm around my grandmother and prayed with her.

The economy took a downturn, and things got difficult in Coeur d'Alene. I lost three good jobs because the companies went out of business. The Big Man closed his store and took a position as the logistics manager for an office supply chain store. It paid better and got him medical insurance. But things didn't look up for the economy. My husband's chain store was going out of business, and we decided we needed to move to a larger city, where there would be more job opportunities for us. I started sending résumés to Seattle, Tacoma, and Portland. I traveled to several interviews and was able to take a position in Portland, Oregon.

We packed up and moved our dachshund, our cockatiel, and an aquarium full of fish to Oregon. We loved going to the ocean and spent many weekends there exploring the coast. We thought we might like to retire somewhere along the Pacific shores, so over the next fifteen years, we drove the entire Oregon coastline from north to south. It truly is a beautiful state, very green with lots of trees. But we were tired of the rain and wanted more sunshine when we retired. We searched homes in California, Arizona, Nevada, and even New Mexico. We waited on the Lord to open that door.

Time went by, and we were making plans to drive to Coeur d'Alene to visit my father and then go on to Great Falls. My grandmother was turning one hundred, and we had planned another big party. She was healthy and doing well. She had moved from her little apartment to an assisted-living facility. We had tried to get her to do that for several years, but she just didn't want to. Once she was there, she loved it and said she wished she had moved in years ago. They had a shuttle that took residents to the doctor or to pick up prescriptions and to the grocery store. They had 24-7 nursing care. A lady came in once a week and did the cleaning. She got three meals a day and could mingle with the other folks anytime she wanted.

Just before we left Portland for Coeur d'Alene, I got a call from my father's wife. He had gotten prostate cancer and had been in and out of the hospital fighting it for two years. The cancer had gotten into his bones and muscle tissue, and he had been in a lot of pain. She said he was bad this time and if we could hurry because he was asking for me.

We left immediately and drove straight through; it took seven hours. When we got to the hospital in Coeur d'Alene, my father had been in so much pain that he was on large doses of morphine and wasn't conscious any longer. I took him in my arms and began to pray, and I told him I was there with him. He died in my arms a few minutes later.

We went on to our grandmother's birthday party then returned to Coeur d'Alene for my father's funeral. Standing at the grave after the service, my big brother quietly said to me, "Well, it looks like we're orphans again." When our mother had moved out and we went to live with our grandparents, the Catholic school we attended was also an orphanage. Because we went there and because our parents were gone, everyone had just assumed that we were orphans too.

I looked at him and smiled and said, "No, we're not. Our grandmother is still with us!"

We hugged each other, but I knew he was grieving the loss of a father that he had wanted badly to have more in his life.

Time went by. After a couple more years, it was getting close to our grandmother's birthday again, and we were making plans to drive back to Montana. She would be 103 years old. Just days before we were going to be there, my big brother called with bad news. Our grandmother had tripped over a rug during the night on her way to the bathroom. She broke her femur, the largest bone in her leg, and was bleeding internally. My brother was a certified EMT and was very clinical about explaining what had happened. I asked what they were going to do about it and if I should come up earlier than we had planned.

He said they usually operate to stop the bleeding and set the broken bone, but our grandmother was only ninety-seven pounds, and even though she was healthy, she was frail. They didn't think she would make it through the surgery and were hoping the bleeding would stop by itself. He didn't think we needed to come up early, and we agreed to wait to hear from him the next day. There wasn't any improvement the next day, and I was torn between changing our plans so we could be there earlier, which my husband and I would do, but it meant telling our bosses that we needed to be gone before the time we had requested off. I was agonizing about what to do when my brother called back. Our grandmother had passed away. I was so angry with myself for not going right away when he had called.

We discussed her wishes to be cremated and buried next to her husband, son, and daughter. We discussed some plans for the funeral. There were many of the friends we had grown up with at the funeral. They came to pay their respects to our grandmother. All her brothers and her sister had already passed, both of her children had passed, and suddenly, my brother and I realized we were the oldest next of kin in the family. It was a beautiful service with a salvation message. We laid her to rest next to our grandfather and her son, with our mother on the other side.

I missed her. As I stood by the graves, I remembered the last time I had the opportunity to stay with her. When we got ready for bed, she asked me if I wanted to pray with her. We used to do the little prayer. "Now I lay me down to sleep. I pray the Lord my soul to keep, but should I die before I wake, I pray my soul the Lord will take."

I realized that although I had prayed with her many times, I hadn't been with her at night to pray before going to bed for a long time. I said I would be honored to pray with her. She went first, and I was immediately humbled by her prayers. She prayed for all the little children in the world and asked God to please protect them tonight and give food to those who were hungry. She prayed for all the sick children in the world and asked the Lord to comfort them and heal them. She prayed that the Lord would send someone to the little children to tell them about Jesus. She prayed for my big brother and his family, she prayed for me and my husband, she prayed for my son and his family, and then she prayed for each of her grandchildren and their families.

She prayed for several other relatives, nieces and nephews, and their children. She prayed for my brother's mother- and father-in-law and several people she knew who were sick. She prayed for some of the neighbors we had lived next to over the years and asked the Lord to bring someone to them to tell them about Jesus. Then she was done.

I was speechless at first and never knew my grandmother had prayed like that. I mumbled something and said amen, and we got into bed. I rolled over and held my grandmother close and told her how humbled I was by her beautiful prayers. I told her I thought she was going to say the little prayer we used to say when we were kids. She laughed and started it, I joined in, and when we had finished, I gave her a kiss on the cheek and told her how much I loved her. I am grateful that I will always have that precious memory.

On the other side of losing someone I loved who was very special to me stood Jesus. Dying is part of life, but when we know the Lord and that our loved ones are with him, we know we will see them again one day. Grief is different for everyone. For me, I cry until I'm out of tears, and then I remember all the good times we had together. I can still see my grandmother pointing the hose from the kitchen sink out the window and soaking my big brother! She loved water fights and usually was the one who started them. Once while we were visiting my mother at the hospital, I bent over to get something off the floor. My grandmother scooped up some ice from a cup on the tray and winked at my husband. He didn't know what she was up to and just kept quiet. She reached over and poured the ice down my pants. My husband laughed right out loud and thought she was just adorable. I'd lived with that growing up with her and took it in stride. My big brother laughed because it wasn't him this time.

In the ten years I lived in Coeur d'Alene, my father and I worked on building a better relationship with each other. I told him how hurt I had been because he never called on my birthday and never even sent a card. On my next birthday, he called and asked if I'd go to lunch with him. It became a special thing that he did every year, and I loved him for it.

CHAPTER 10

◈

My sister-in-law, my brother's wife, was a beautiful person, and I loved talking about what the Lord was teaching us when we were together. She had a depth of knowledge about many spiritual things, and she loved sharing with others. She gave me a recipe for a winter-tea mix that I have always loved. I can't handle caffeine and started drinking decaf teas years ago, so we shared different ideas for tea mixes and flavors. She had been diagnosed with breast cancer and was trying to follow a healthy diet. I had an opportunity to travel to Montana, not my usual area at work, but I was covering for another human resources adviser who was on vacation. I traveled up during the week, handled the issues the next day, and on Friday after work, I drove up to the ranch to visit with my big brother and my sister-in-law. It was wintertime, and there was snow on the ground. I had decent weather, even sunshine, and it was good to see my mountains again.

On the way to the ranch, I tuned the radio in my rental car to one of the Christian stations in the area. I sang along and was worshipping the Lord and having a blessed day. A song came on that they said was brand-new, that they had never played before. It was incredible! It was by David Crowder and was simply called, "I Am." He sang,

> There's no place that his love can't reach.
> There's no place where we can't find peace. There's
> no end to amazing grace. Take me in with your
> arms spread wide. Take me in like an orphaned
> child. Never let go. Never leave my side.

I had goose bumps all up and down my arms. I was certain he had written this and was singing it just for me. The chorus said, "I am holding on to you! I am holding on to you! In the middle of the storm, I am holding on. I am." I realized this could be taken more than one way. It could be the Lord saying to me that he was holding on to me, or it could be me saying to the Lord that I was holding on to him.

The second verse says,

> Love like this, oh my God to find. I am overwhelmed. What a joy divine. Love like this sets our hearts on fire. This is my resurrection song. This is my hallelujah come. This is why it's to you I run. There's no space that his love can't reach. There's no place where we can't find peace. There's no end to amazing grace.

I told my brother and his wife about it when I got to the ranch. They hadn't heard it yet. We had a wonderful time visiting and praying together. I walked over and visited with Grandma, the woman who used to be my mother-in-law from my first marriage. Since she was my brother's wife's mother, she lived there with them on the ranch. I enjoyed getting to see her again and gave her my love, and we prayed together before I left.

I was at work when my brother called me. He was in Seattle at the hospital. They had tried giving my sister-in-law some new cocktail of chemicals to battle her breast cancer. She had a terrible reaction; it was like the chemicals were burning her skin off from the inside out. They had flown her from Montana in a medical helicopter to the burn center in the Seattle hospital because they were better equipped to handle this kind of issue.

I said I was on my way. I called my boss and explained what had happened and said I would continue to take calls and took my laptop to keep working. I drove home and explained to my husband what was happening, I grabbed my suitcase and threw some clothes together and said I'd call him when I got there and found out more.

It was a four-hour drive from my home to the hospital. My brother had told me which wing they were in, but it was a big place and took asking for directions to find them. When I came out of the elevator and saw my big brother across the lobby, I ran to him. We just held each other tightly for a few minutes. Then he said to go on in the room and say hello.

The odor in the room gagged me. My sister-in-law was lying on her back, and they were changing her sheets. It was causing her pain, and they were doing their best to be careful. I stood back and prayed for her and waited until they were finished.

One of the nurses came over to me and apologized. She said my sister-in-law's body was leaking fluids so rapidly that they couldn't keep her bed dry. I noticed huge piles of wet sheets on the floor and realized that was where the odor was coming from. The chemicals had burned her skin off, so she had nothing to keep the body fluids in. They said they were going to try a new type of skin graft the next morning to see if it would help her retain more fluid. My brother had told me that touching her anywhere caused her pain.

I walked over after the nurses had all left and had taken the dirty sheets out. I softly called her name, and she opened her eyes and smiled at me. I told her I was there with her and my brother and her youngest daughter, who had come on the helicopter with her. I told her I was praying and asked if she wanted me to pray with her. She nodded slightly, so I prayed out loud, leaning over by her ear.

We took turns sitting in the room with her. My brother had brought a small CD player and was playing some of her favorite Christian music near her head. They gave her something for pain and to sleep, so I suggested we go get something to eat and find a motel at my treat. When we got into our room, my niece wanted to take a shower, and my brother wanted to go back to the hospital. I gave him my car and a room key and said I'd stay with my niece.

The next day was difficult. My sister-in-law was in surgery for a long time. Unfortunately, the skin graft wasn't working. And her organs had started to shut down. The doctors met with us and gave us the sad news. They didn't feel there was any hope for any kind of recovery. My sister-in-law was going in and out of consciousness. We still took turns being with her and letting her know we were there. The doctors told us to expect her to pass within twenty-four hours. She died later that night. My big brother had just lost the love of his life, and I felt unable to comfort him. He had held on for so long that the Lord would perform a miracle, and he'd bring his wife back home to the ranch. I prayed for him and my nieces and nephew.

We held a beautiful celebration of life back in Great Falls. I saw many members of the family I hadn't seen since I was divorced from my first husband. My big brother had asked me if I could take care of Grandma because he had his three children to take care of during the service. Grandma, my sister-in-law's mother, was the woman who had also been my mother-in-law for eighteen years when I was married to her son. When it was time to go in, she reached for my hand with tears in her eyes. We sat together and handed each other tissues. She had buried her husband, her mother and father, her sister, and now her daughter. She was grieving.

Several pastors spoke beautifully about my sister-in-law. The seven-hour drive back home was lonely. It wasn't too much longer before I got another call from my big brother. Grandma had gotten COVID-19 and had passed away. We had been so close for so many years. I felt the loss immediately. Because of COVID-19, they weren't able to hold any kind of service. I grieved alone and far from my family.

After I had returned to work, I was having more pain in my lower back. I had a position that required that I traveled almost three weeks out of four, driving between two and five hours a day. When I hauled my suitcases out to my car, it hurt. When I got to my hotel and hauled my suitcases out of the car and into my room, it hurt. I had gone to a back specialist two years before and was set up for physical-therapy sessions. I got the therapist to teach me several exercises that I could do when I traveled. The exercises had helped, but I have pain in my neck and lower back from having motorcycle accidents and taking a couple of bad falls snow skiing.

Now, I was told I was full of arthritis and the exercises were designed to help. The pain in my hands got so bad that the minute I got into my hotel rooms, I'd spend half an hour soaking my hands in hot water in the bathroom sink because the arthritis hurt so bad after holding the steering wheel for so long. I eventually had to have surgery on both hands, and it helped reduce the pain.

After getting to my office each day, I could do good for three or four hours. The pain was always there in my back. If I dropped something on the floor, it stayed there because it hurt too much to bend over to pick it up. I took in an ergonomic back pillow my physical therapist suggested to use in my office chair. I took a heating pad to work. I was doing everything I could to work through the pain. It would get so bad by lunch time that I had to use a cane to get down the hall to the women's bathroom. I was taking extrastrength arthritis Tylenol to get through the afternoon.

When it was time to go home, I could barely walk to the elevator to get from my office on the second floor to the first floor. Then I had to walk across the driveway in front of our building to get to my car. The seat in my car was helpful, but I had an hour's drive, sometimes more with bad traffic, to get home when I wasn't traveling. When I pulled into our driveway, my husband would come out to help me get out of the car and into the house. I spent the evening lying in a recliner with a heating pad. My husband does the cooking and would already have something ready for dinner. I would take more Tylenol and go to bed. The physical therapist had gotten me into swimming. I could swim laps for an hour, and it helped. But managing the pain became too much, and I made an appointment with the back specialist I had seen before.

After having a CAT scan on my back, the doctor showed us the pictures. I had five damaged vertebrae in my lower back, all with bulging disks. The doctor explained my options. Typically, they give cortisone shots for one or two damaged vertebrae to reduce the pain. Unfortunately, because I had five damaged vertebrae, they couldn't give me that much cortisone because the body can only take certain amounts.

The doctor explained that they usually could fuse one or two and three vertebrae together but not five. They would have to actually fuse seven together, and that would do two things: (1) it would render me totally stiff and unable to bend at all, and (2) fusing seven vertebrae together would cause the top and the bottom ones to become damaged because of the additional pressure and stress, and I'd be in a wheelchair for the rest of my life. I'd been told when I was twenty-seven and had gone to the knee surgeon that I would be in a wheelchair by the time I was thirty. That didn't happen then, and I wasn't going to let it happen now. I was going to research everything I could about this and find a solution.

The doctor sent me to see a pain-management specialist to look at two other feasible options. After reviewing my records and giving me an exam, the doctor told me about the two procedures he used for pain management in my circumstances. The first one, which he did not recommend for me, involved a complex system of painfully removing cells from the larger bones in my body and growing actual tissue that would be reinserted into the damaged vertebrae to repair the damage. It seemed to work best with young athletes who could recover quickly.

The second procedure was to open between six and ten holes in my back right next to my spinal cord and burn the ends of the nerves with a laser. I had no choice. I couldn't sit at my desk without tremendous pain, I couldn't travel without tremendous pain, and I couldn't walk without tremendous pain. I agreed to have the procedure. My insurance company said that the procedure was very risky and would only cover it after the doctor performed two test procedures first. He would open the holes in my back and numb the nerve endings he would perform the laser procedure on. If I had less pain after both test procedures, they would cover the actual procedure with the laser.

I was terrified and kept repeating scriptures and praying to myself. I recited two of my favorite scriptures:

> This is the day the Lord has made. Rejoice
> and be glad in it! (Psalm 118:24)

> The Lord is my shepherd, I will lack noth-
> ing. He makes me lie down in green pastures, he
> leads me beside quiet waters, he restores my soul.

He guides me in paths of righteousness for his name's sake. Even though I walk through the valley of the shadow of death, I will fear no evil for you are with me, your rod and your staff comfort me. You prepare a table before me in the presence of my enemies. You anoint my head with oil, my cup overflows. Surely goodness and love will follow me all the days of my life, and I will dwell in the house of the Lord forever. (Psalm 23)

I was awake through the entire test process, and they wouldn't give me anything for pain because I had to tell them when I felt them numbing the nerves. It was so painful that I almost didn't go back for the second test. I cried all the way to the clinic and didn't want to go inside. My husband kept telling me that the numbing had reduced the pain in my back, and I could move better, so it was worth going through the second test. I hated every moment, cried, gritted my teeth, sweated bullets, and when I got through, my husband took me for a Big Mac and an ice-cold Pepsi.

The actual laser procedure would have to be set up for two different weeks. He would do one side of the spinal cord one week and the other side of my spinal cord the next week. Because this was a surgical procedure, I wasn't able to continue swimming until my skin fully healed. I knew that I was becoming terribly anxious and stressed and scared about how painful this was going to be. I prayed and cried and read scriptures. The day of the first procedure, I knew that I was covered by his precious hedge of protection (Job 1:10 and Psalm 125:2) and that I was blessed and that he would be with me. I didn't do very well, and the doctor had to stop the procedure several times for a few minutes to let me calm down. I was crying so hard, I guess I was shaking, and he couldn't have me moving when he was holding a laser in my body. I got through it. The Lord was faithful to bless me and help my stress.

The second procedure went better. They decided to give me something to calm me down, and that helped. We got through that session faster and without me becoming hysterical. I went home and rested.

The next day, it was clear that I wasn't having as much pain as I'd had before. I could only hope it would last longer than what the doctor said it would. He told me that it could last over six months or more. It didn't. Four months later, the pain came screaming back. My husband had retired and agreed to drive me on the next trip I needed to take for work. My company reimbursed me for the gas we used in the car and for my meals and the hotel room. I was incredibly grateful for his kindness and got a lot accomplished. I could recline the seat in the car, so it didn't hurt so much while my husband did the driving. We took another trip before the holidays, and I got to visit every center in the four states that my area covered. When I was back in my office at my home center, I would have to manage the pain throughout the day. After spending too many days sitting day after day, the pain was becoming intolerable again.

I had requested and received permission to work from home. I could take all my calls on my company cell phone and had my company laptop to complete any work required while I could sit in my recliner without pain. This was during the spread of COVID-19, and both my husband and I were in high-risk categories, so working from home was an important health issue for me.

About this time, I got a phone call from my little cousin who used to ski with us. He and his sister were together because their mother had gotten COVID-19 and passed away. They knew she was always special to me and wanted to let me know. Because of COVID-19, they weren't going to have any kind of a funeral. I expressed my sympathy for their loss and thanked them for letting me know. I had been to his home just a few months before when I found out where he lived. It had been so good to visit with him. He had told me that his mother was in an assisted-living home near him, and I had wanted to visit her, but COVID-19 hit, and nobody was allowed to visit. This was a big hole in my heart that day. How do you grieve for someone who was so special to you, but because of COVID-19, you can't travel to be with family or even hold a service to say goodbye?

The pain in my back had become unendurable again. It was obviously time to retire. I was sixty-eight and ready, and I wasn't going to go through all that stress and pain to have the nerve endings laser burned again, and it cost too much to get less than a four-month period of relief.

I knew that the Lord had been telling me for years to write a book about what had happened to me and how I was saved. I wasn't sure I could get a book published like that. It is very personal and intense, so I wrote a historical adventure story, and it got published. I sold a few books. I put off writing my testimony story for years, because I was too busy working, because I was always tired and sore when I got home, because I always had house cleaning and laundry and errands on the weekends, because it hurt too much to sit for longer than a few minutes at a desk to type, and every excuse that passed across my mind. I am deeply sorry about that.

Once I retired, I couldn't use the excuses about being tired from working and being sore. I learned to type on a laptop while I'm sitting in a recliner—no pain! There is a swimming pool two blocks away where I can do laps, and I have a hot tub that helps with arthritis pain and stiffness. I still have the exercises I learned from the physical therapist, and I can manage the pain most of the time, so this is the book that the Lord asked me to write. Jesus did not say, "I will drag you along with me." He said, "Follow me."

CHAPTER 11

This book was written for any woman who has had an abortion. My prayer for you is that the scriptures I have shared that released me from guilt, shame, remorse, and fear after I realized that the abortions I had took the life of my first two children will release you. I pray that the Lord will bring you to your knees so you can ask him to forgive you, so that you will also experience his grace when He heals your heart and renews your soul. Remember, Psalm 118:5 says, "In my anguish I cried to the Lord and He answered by setting me free." He set me free, and He will do the same for you.

This book is also for any man who got a woman pregnant and helped her have an abortion. You were somebody's father. Whether you paid for the abortion or not, your child was alive and living until she had the abortion. The Bible calls having sex with someone you are not married to the sin of lasciviousness, which is defined as having a lustful or lewd purpose, the act of sexual immorality. In Acts 15:29, it says that "you are to abstain from…sexual immorality." First Corinthians 6:18 tells us to "flee from sexual immorality." In 1 Corinthians 10:8, we are admonished that "we should not commit sexual immorality." Sexual immorality is fornication, having sex with someone you are not married to. You need to go to your knees and ask the Lord to forgive your sin(s). Then ask the Lord to forgive you for helping the woman you got pregnant to have an abortion, which took the life of your child. Then live what 1 Corinthians 10:13 promises you that "God is faithful; he will not let you be tempted beyond what you can bear. But when you are tempted, he will also provide a way out so that you can stand up under it." What an incredible promise to us!

Ladies, these scriptures pertain to you too. Lasciviousness, lust, lewdness, sexual immorality, and fornication are not just a sin of men. Proverbs 6:24–25 warns men to "keep away from immoral women, from the smooth tongue of the wayward wife. Do not lust in your heart after her beauty or let her captivate you with her eyes." The apostle Paul wrote in Galatians 5:19–21, warning them not to gratify the desires of a sinful nature! He told them,

> The acts of a sinful nature are obvious: sexual immorality, impurity, debauchery; idolatry and witchcraft; hatred, discord, jealousy, fits of rage, selfish ambition, dissentions, factions and envy; drunkenness, orgies, and the like. I warn you, as I did before, that those who live like this will not inherit the kingdom of God.

He goes on in Galatians 5:22–23 to tell us, "The fruit of the Spirit is love, joy, peace, patience, kindness, goodness, faithfulness, gentleness and self-control." If you have been born again, the Holy Spirit will be with you and will guide you. What Paul is saying here is that the proof of the fruit of the Holy Spirit is the opposite of a sinful nature.

Another letter from the apostle Paul is in 1 Thessalonians 4:7 and says,

> It is God's will that you should be holy; that you should avoid sexual immorality, that each of you should learn to control his own body in a way that is holy and honorable; not in passionate lust like the heathen who do not know God… for God did not call us to be impure, but to live a holy life.

I haven't spoken about Satan, and there are a few misconceptions I want to talk about. Satan is not all-powerful like God is. He can't be everywhere like God can. He can only be in one place at a time. He can't read your mind. He can't tell the future. He doesn't have superpowers. God created him. He is nothing more than a fallen angel. The book of Revelation tells us that he started a war in heaven, rebelling against God. He was defeated, and Satan and all the angels who had followed him were cast out of heaven and thrown into hell, out of God's presence. Being out of God's presence and being subject to Satan's anger and sent to hell have turned the beautiful, majestic angels God created into hideous demons.

Satan has only one goal—to hurt God. If he can get a human being to die before they are born again, he knows that will hurt God because God loved that person and made a way for them to be with him. Scripture tells us that babies and young children who die will go to heaven. If a child hasn't yet reached the age of accountability, they go to heaven. Accountability means a person knows that they have committed a sin and must ask God for forgiveness. This is different for every person, and God knows whether they understand. Satan uses whatever he can to get people to turn from anything that might bring them closer to God.

In the years that I have been ministering to women who have had abortions, I found that many of them have succumbed to being addicted to smoking, alcohol, and/or drugs, attempting to find a release from the constant overwhelming guilt, remorse, shame, nightmares, or thoughts of suicide. Many of us will do anything to make it stop hurting. I shared with you that I had put every thought about my abortions into a black box and hid it in my heart. I tied it up tight, securing it so nobody and nothing could open it, because opening it meant facing what was in that box, and that hurt too much. It was only when I had faith that Jesus loved me that I was able to open that box with him, remove it from my heart, and receive the Lord's blessings. You might have heard before someone saying, "Let go and let God." First John 1:9 tells us, "If we confess our sins, he is faithful and just and will forgive us our sins and purify us from all unrighteousness." I have blessings for every one of you struggling with any addiction.

Let's start with cigarettes. I smoked off and on for many years. I tried to quit over and over. I prayed every prayer and claimed every promise in the Bible. I had people lay hands on me and pray for me. And I'd be able to not smoke for a long time (over a year), but sometimes, the body wants what it wants, and it wants it *now*. Get a Bible. There are hundreds of promises from God that you can find. If you are married, pray with your spouse and ask them to pray for you. If you attend a church, go to your pastor and ask for prayer. It always helps to know when others care enough to pray for you.

But in the end, it comes down to you and Jesus. If you have been born again, then you know how to go to him and ask him for help. If you are not born-again, why aren't you? Go back and read chapters 5 and 6 again. For me, after I tried the gum and the patches and the pills—and nothing worked—I went to Jesus and simply said, "I don't want to smoke. Please help me to quit."

Guess what Jesus said to me? He said, "Then why do you keep a pack of cigarettes in the house? If you want to be a nonsmoker, stop acting like you're a smoker."

I had thrown away all the cigarettes before, but I had always kept the pretty little flowered cigarette case I'd bought and the slim silver lighter with a few cigarettes just in case. I cleared out everything, tossed the cigarette case and all the lighters I could find in the car, in the house—everywhere. With the last of them in my hands, I walked to the garbage can, tossed them in, and said out loud, "I am *not* a smoker." That was the last day I smoked, and that was over twenty years ago. I chose to be a nonsmoker. I chose to be healthier because my body is a temple for the Holy Spirit. I pray that anyone who wants to quit smoking will do so right now—today—this minute. I pray that the Lord will bless you fully and that you will walk closer to him for making this choice.

Okay, let's talk about alcohol. Did you know that Jesus's first miracle was to change water into wine? Obviously, Jesus drank wine. There are many scriptures in the Bible that talk about drinking, and there are many scriptures that admonish us not to be drunk. Remember, in Galatians 5, Paul warned us to keep away from drunkenness. Ephesians 5:15–18 says,

> Be very careful how you live – not as unwise,
> but be wise, making the most out of every oppor-
> tunity...therefore, do not be foolish but under-

stand what the Lord's will is. Do not get drunk
which leads to debauchery.

Debauchery is sexual immorality.

And in Romans 13:13, it says, "Let us behave decently, as in the daytime, not as in orgies and drunkenness and sexual immorality and debauchery, not in dissention and jealousy." The Bible does not say you can't drink alcohol. It says don't be drunk. If you have been using alcohol to ease the pain, take the pain away, disappear into oblivion, or just because you don't want to hurt, I want to say this to you: God is bigger than your pain. God is more powerful than your hurt, and God loves you. He doesn't want you to hurt. He wants to take your pain away. He created you to be a beautiful, thriving child of God, blessed by his grace, saved by faith in Jesus, filled with his precious Holy Spirit to guide and protect you. You have a choice to continue as you have in drunkenness, or allow the Lord to help you. Find a local Alcoholics Anonymous; find a meeting close to you and go. I have worked with Alcoholics Anonymous and Al-Anon, the support group for spouses of alcoholics, for many years. If you are serious about making the choice to quit drinking, you can do it with God's help.

Recovering from being addicted to pain pills, codeine, cocaine, crack, Ecstasy, methamphetamine, heroin, LSD, mescaline, PCP (phenylcyclohexyl piperidine), opioids, and cannabis (marijuana) is possible. Contact any local rehabilitation clinic; discuss if your insurance will cover your care. There are many faith-based organizations available to help you. Some have recovered addicts as counselors; they know what you're going through and how to help you best. Don't wait. Do it now. Get professional help. Let go and let God help you. There are so many examples of the Lord delivering his people.

The Lord is my rock, my fortress and my
deliverer. (2 Samuel 2:22)

God reached down from on high and took
hold of me; he drew me out of deep waters. He

rescued me from my powerful enemy. (Psalm 18:16)

God has delivered us from a deadly peril. On him we have set our hope that He will continue to deliver us. (2 Corinthians 1:10)

Rejoice in suffering because we know that suffering produces perseverance. Perseverance produces character, and character produces hope. And hope does not disappoint us, because God has poured out his love into our hearts by the Holy Spirit, whom he has given us. (Romans 5:3–5)

In my anguish, I cried to the Lord, and he answered by setting me free. (Psalm 118:5)

If you are having horrible nightmares, night terrors, or bad dreams about your abortion, you could be suffering from post-traumatic stress disorder (PTSD). PTSD can be dormant for years until an event, a smell, a picture, or anything triggers it. Talk to your doctor and explain what is happening to you. Seek professional help from a counselor, therapist, or pastor.

I will lie down and sleep; I will wake again because the Lord sustains me. (Psalm 3:5)

I will lie down and sleep in peace, for you alone O Lord, make me dwell in safety. (Psalm 4:8)

When you lie down, you will not be afraid; when you lie down your sleep will be sweet. (Proverbs 3:24)

If you are having thoughts of suicide, please know how precious and loved you are. First Corinthians 6:20 reminds you that "you are not your own; you have been bought at a price." The price you were bought for was God's only Son, Jesus Christ. Remember the song by Crowder "I Am"? He sings that there's no place that God's love can't reach. There's no place where we can't find peace. There's no end to amazing grace. That means that God is there no matter what is going on to cause those thoughts, and He has a better life for you. All you need to do is ask him. No matter what you're dealing with, God's power is greater. He loves you so much! He loves you enough to send his only Son to the cross to die for you. And nothing is more powerful than giving your life to Jesus and becoming a child of God—being born again, washed clean by Jesus's sacrifice for you.

Call your pastor if you have one. If you don't have one, you can find one online. Call a local counselor or therapist. You can call the national support line by dialing 988. My prayer for you is that the Lord will make himself known to you and that you will pray for being born again and Spirit filled. With the Holy Spirit guiding you, I can promise you that you will find peace.

Anyone who did pray to be born again and have become a new Christian, praise the Lord! It is important that you find fellowship at a church that believes in being born again, and they will support you as you grow in Christ.

And lastly, I want to speak to any doctor who has performed abortions and any nurse who has assisted with abortions. Proverbs 6:16–19 speaks to you and what you are doing and says, "There are six things that the Lord hates, seven that are detestable to him."

1. Haughty eyes
2. A lying tongue
3. *Hands that shed innocent blood*
4. A heart that devises wicked schemes
5. Feet that are quick to rush into evil
6. A false witness who pours out lies
7. And a man who stirs up dissension among brothers

If you're going to say that a woman has the right to her own body, I agree; she does. But the innocent child she is carrying is *not her body*. Her child could have a completely different blood type than its mother. She could be pregnant with a male child. She is not a male, so his body is not hers. If she is pregnant with a female child, that little girl has a separate body from her mother's. When you perform any abortion, you are shedding innocent blood because that child did not have a chance to plead for its own life. You are allowing the mother to choose to kill her innocent baby. We are commanded, "You shall not kill."

If you're going to tell me it's just a blob of tissue, I ask you, how many times have you seen tiny fingers and tiny toes in your bloody tissues? Tiny heads with hair, eyes, noses, mouths, and ears? In April of 1965, *Life* magazine put a picture of an eighteen-week-old human fetus on their cover. There were incredible photographs along with the article titled, "Drama of Life Before Birth" by Lennart Nilsson. The photographs made it so clear that the unborn fetus was a living human being long before s/he was born.

If you're going to say that it isn't a baby until it is born, I was born three months premature. Was I a nonhuman? If I was a human child for the three months that I should have been inside my mother's womb, why wouldn't I be a human child for those same three months if I had been in her womb? There was nothing changed in my body from when I was in the womb when my mother was six months pregnant to when I wasn't in the womb. I was a living human baby girl in the womb, and I was a living human baby girl when they pulled me out of the womb and saved my life.

The following quotes are from James T. Burtchaell's book *Rachel Weeping: The Case Against Abortion*:

> My position is that no one should have the
> right or power to decide what qualities or what
> usefulness others must have to avoid being killed.
> It is enough to be *any* human being, no matter
> how burdensome or troublesome, to merit the
> right to life. (page 322)

Abortion, then—the willful and violent killing of an unborn human being—is homicide... the killing of a human. (page 322)

One cannot fairly allow a child to be destroyed because he or she was conceived by rape or incest, without also allowing the elimination of illegitimate children. (page 322)

My argument is straight forward. Abortion is homicide: the destruction of a child. Save for the rare, rare instance when it is a mortal threat to a mother's life to carry her child to birth, there is no abortion that is not the unjust taking of another's life because it is a burden to one's own. (page 322)

In opposing it, I am in no way insensitive to the plight of mothers who are frightened thirteen-year-olds, or are supporting six children on welfare, or are having to drop out of college because of one night's foolishness. I simply say that these are not misfortunes that justify anyone in raising his or her hand to kill. (page 322)

I want no part of the insanity that sends police into the privacy of homes to stop parents from battering and scalding their four-month-old babies to death, and then uses the same force of law to guarantee the "privacy" of parents to dismember their babies four months before birth. (page 323)

I have no stomach for a society which sees that in many of its home's children are unwanted and would rather exterminate the children than heal the parents. (page 323)

Doctors performing abortions and the nurses assisting them need to go to your knees and beg God's forgiveness. You who have shed innocent blood have no justification to do so. Stop! Stop doing abortions. Walk away. How much money is the next child's life worth to you? In Galatians 5, we read, "I warn you, as I did before, that those who live like this will not inherit the kingdom of God." Why would you be willing to sacrifice *your eternity in heaven* with Jesus to continue to perform abortions?

You have a choice to make. My prayer for you is that the Lord will prepare your heart and that you will choose to stop performing abortions or assisting the doctor who performs them and that you will go to your knees and humbly seek his forgiveness. I pray for you to receive Jesus as your Savior, that you will be born again and Spirit filled and receive the blessings from the Lord that you were created for.

In Deuteronomy 19:9–10, Moses tells us, "Love the Lord your God and walk always in his ways...do this so that innocent blood will not be shed in your land...and so you will not be guilty of bloodshed."

On the other side of the following:

- Abuse and neglect by my own mother
- Abandonment by my mother and my father
- Believing there was something terribly wrong with me
- Believing whatever it was that was wrong with me meant nobody would ever love me
- Being adopted by my grandparents so our mother couldn't take us away
- Witnessing my mother after she was battered, brutalized, and beaten
- Being hurt and confused why my mother chose to return to a violent man instead of being with her own children
- Puberty

- Developing into a shapely young woman unsure of how to handle that
- Being confused about the attention I got from guys—did they see what it was that was so terribly wrong with me and just ignore it, or did they not see anything wrong with me?
- Being desperate to be loved, using sex while knowing that sex wasn't love
- Being attacked and abused by a doctor I thought I could trust
- Having an illegal abortion when I was just sixteen years old
- Losing all self-confidence and believing I had done the worst thing a girl could do
- Getting pregnant a second time and having a second illegal abortion when I was just eighteen years old
- Realizing I needed to confess my sins and asking God to forgive me
- Realizing Jesus loved me just as I was who I was and that there really wasn't anything wrong with me except that I needed Jesus in my life
- Giving my life to Jesus, becoming born again, being baptized in the Holy Spirit
- Understanding that I had allowed my first two children to be killed to have two abortions "to solve my problems"
- Following the Lord into a ministry to help women who were struggling after having an abortion
- Following the Lord into a ministry educating junior high and high school students about what abortions really are and what happens when you have one
- Following the Lord into a radio talk show ministry about pro-life issues
- Following the Lord into a ministry writing a Christian pro-life newspaper column
- Losing the ministries the Lord brought to me
- Getting a divorce

- Falling in love with a man of God who has remained faithful, honest, kind, compassionate, caring, giving, loving, and wonderful
- Experiencing three knee surgeries and finally getting a full knee replacement
- Experiencing excruciating pain from five damaged vertebrae in my lower back and the only option open to me to relieve the constant pain
- Experiencing the pain of arthritis in my hands so badly, they both needed surgery
- Experiencing the pain of arthritis in my neck, my shoulders, my elbows, and my back and learning how to live a blessed life with the Lord
- Retiring
- Following the Lord's direction to write a book that offers help to others who might be struggling after having an abortion

On the other side of all these things were the Lord's grace and love; Jesus's sacrifice, forgiveness, and my rebirth; being baptized by the Holy Spirit; and becoming a new person. I'm nobody special. I'm just a girl who made some bad choices that I will have to live with for the rest of my life. Yes, there were some bad things that happened to me, but those things don't define me. And with the Lord's forgiveness and my willingness to search for the answers, Jesus brought me to the cross to prove how much He loved me when I thought I couldn't be loved. It happened to me, and it can happen to you.

My prayer for you is that you seek the Lord, ask Jesus to come into your life as your Savior, ask the Lord to baptize you with his precious Holy Spirit, and walk the blessed life he created for you to live.

www.ingramcontent.com/pod-product-compliance
Lightning Source LLC
Chambersburg PA
CBHW022021150726
47990CB00002B/754